POPULAR
SINGING

Learner Services

Please return
on or before
the last date
stamped below

CITY COLLEGE
NORWICH

2 4 APR 2009

2 0 APR 2010

1 1 MAY 2010

1 6 FEB 2011

1 3 JAN 2012

1 3 JAN 2012

3 1 JAN 2012

2 8 FEB 2012

1 3 NOV 2013

D0539367

POPULAR SINGING

A PRACTICAL GUIDE TO: POP, JAZZ, BLUES, ROCK, COUNTRY AND GOSPEL

DONNA SOTO-MORETTINI

A & C BLACK · LONDON

First published 2006

A & C Black Publishers Limited
38 Soho Square
London W1D 3HB
www.acblack.com

ISBN 0 7136 7266 8

A CIP catalogue record for this book is available from the British Library.

A & C Black uses paper produced with elemental chlorine-free pulp, harvested from managed sustainable forests.

Illustrations by Earl Soto

Typeset in 10/13pt Bembo

Printed and bound in Great Britain by
J. H. Haynes & Co. Ltd., Sparkford

CONTENTS

Acknowledgements

For their continuing help and encouragement over the last few years I'd like to thank Lise Olson and Gillyanne Kayes. I owe heartfelt thanks to Sarah Stephenson for a close, critical and very helpful reading of the first chapters of the manuscript. Nick Phillips, Dror Mohar, Kim Planert and Jon Thornton generously gave time, talent and space to help out in the recording process. I owe a great debt of gratitude to Sir Paul McCartney for being so liberal with his time and so open in interview, and to Mark Featherstone-Witty for brokering the deal.

I am grateful to Alexandra, Alanna, Bijan, Kenny and Nina for influencing my listening habits in the best possible ways – often without knowing it.

Finally, I owe the greatest debt to my many students at Central, LIPA and the RSAMD for their patience, their generosity and their inspirational vocal talents!

This book is for my Dad who first played Sinatra for me.

Introduction

Sometimes I love beautiful voices. I respond to the purity of Karen Carpenter's great rich autumnal tones. I appreciate the crisp, fluid and lucid quality of Ella Fitzgerald's voice, or the earthy, almost funereal and haunting depths of Paul Robeson's. But my real passion lies elsewhere, because as much as I love beautiful voices, I am more fervently in awe of the whole of the spectrum of sound that the human voice can make – and I love that great spectrum even more when it is employed honestly in the service of heartfelt musical communication. Flaws, warts, scratches, creaks, rumbles, screams, whispers, shouts, wails, sighs, grit, gravel and even dodgy intonation can move my heart when the artist has something deep and immediate to communicate.

Maybe my love of these artless sounds has to do with my general love of breaking the rules in the pursuit of frankly passionate expression. Perhaps it is to do with valuing the sense of abandon that so few of us ever manage to achieve in our day-to-day lives. Perhaps it is partly simple admiration for artists who go their own way in spite of the good advice of others. No doubt it has something to do with the desire to hear things I've not heard before or to glimpse ever so briefly into the heart of someone else through their singing. But it must also be that the voice gets right to heart of who we are – and when singers are defiant, and different, and bold, and passionate, they are both refusing to conform to imposed standards and at the same time insisting that it is in the great variety of individual human life and sound that we can discover what really matters. This book is the result of my explorations into the way that these two vocal realms – the wild & defiant vs. the pure & the beautiful – seem to 'clash' so often in vocal performance and, of course, in the approach to teaching vocalists.

This is a book about style. It is a book for vocalists, voice teachers and people who are interested in the varieties and the evolution of contemporary popular vocal styles. It is not a history book; nor is it, strictly speaking, a comprehensive book about vocal style, which would include much more in the way of history and context. It is a practical book that aims to concentrate on the performance and practice of popular singing. My method is to isolate and describe where possible the elements of popular singing, and to consider how one might learn and teach these elements. As far as I know, there is no other book that sets out to do this. This is a very different kind of experience from that normally had through traditional vocal tuition, or through books on how to train your voice. From the outset, I will attempt to be clear about an area (popular singing/music) that doesn't often seem to invite much clarity in written analysis.

Most definitions of popular music – and they aren't easy to find – are couched in some pretty careful language. Doubtless this is because as with most other art forms, boundaries don't remain fixed for long. Most forms grow and change through the blending and blurring of categories, and singing styles in this century have certainly followed this pattern. For some, Musical Theatre repertoire represents a branch of popular music, whereas for most singers, Musical Theatre is considered 'legit' and best approached through classical or traditional teaching methods.

To add to the confusion, many singers, over the span of their careers, choose to explore songs in multiple styles or genres, and this can increase the confusion over something as seemingly simple as what kind of music one is listening to. When Barbra Streisand sings a Rock song, are you really listening to Rock music? I would argue that you're not – you're listening to Barbra Streisand – but that argument would be based squarely on the strength of Streisand's style, which doesn't alter significantly between a standard show tune and a contemporary Rock ballad.

One of the difficulties of approaching this subject is in trying to be clear about the difference between style and genre, and I am probably on safest ground if I begin by claiming this distinction as my own. The elements of vocal style that we will be covering here are a series of vocal 'choices' made by the artist. Some of them are choices that aren't available to all of us – few singers can successfully prolong the effort-level or 'constricted' onset sound of Tina Turner, or match the extended improvisational ability of Stevie Wonder. For others, however, it isn't the limitation of their abilities that necessarily determines the choices they make. Many singers, in fact, have a rather narrow band of stylistic choices that they work through and of course, that *is* their style (think of Sade, for instance). Others make few but strong choices that leave their imprint unmistakably (Billie Holiday and Karen Carpenter come to mind). Some have an extraordinary range of choices that seem adaptable to any number of song styles (Paul McCartney and Billy Joel are great examples of this).

These choices are what I will be analysing and describing as 'the elements

of style'. Genre is a more difficult thing, since you can't find two Jazz musicians who will give you the same definition of Jazz. Nor will you find two
musicians who can agree on the difference between Rhythm & Blues and
Soul or even, simply, the Blues. Like most musicians, I've grown up alongside
players who seemed to be speaking the same language as me, and we seemed
to have a workable shorthand vocabulary. As a young singer working in
California, I was aware that we often used descriptions that gave us a kind of
common ground to work from. These descriptions aren't quite as useful in
England, where a 'valley sound' or a 'Motown feel' doesn't have the same
currency. There are, of course, distinctions that have to be made by large
companies who sell recordings, but these often seem as unhelpful as the
academic music studies I've looked through: the best they can do is create
large general categories and then hope that their staff and their customers
have enough local knowledge to find that Lyle Lovett CD.

In popular music, at the very beginning of the recording industry, the first
strong, detectable popular genres were Blues and Jazz. As Jazz branched out
into many distinct subcategories, from the big swing bands to bebop, and
through to more progressive forms, Blues remained more or less a 'shading'
that infiltrated nearly every style of popular music. While Folk music has a
long and wonderful history, 'Country' music – which might have been seen
in its early days as a marketable brand of Folk music, but which owes as much
to the Blues – quickly found its own distinctions and began to influence
other forms once recordings were widely available. With the beginnings of
'rock' or 'rockabilly' music in the early 1950s, elements of Jazz, Blues and
Country were all detectable. Throughout this book, my interest in these
histories will centre only on how such things influenced the stylistic choices
made by singers working and recording at the time.

In the late part of this century, when one thinks of vocalists, there are still
large categorical distinctions – but of course, these distinctions are only
marginally helpful. We may have a general notion of what Country singers
sound like (which grows a bit more confused when we listen to KD Lang or
Shania Twain), or of what Jazz singers sound like (although up until the
massive success of Norah Jones, many people would have been able to think
of only few contemporary Jazz singers since Jazz fusion styles have so successfully blurred this category), or of what Folk singers sound like (although
applying the label to someone as unique as Damien Rice can be pretty
confusing), but it is often just as easy to let the recording companies sort it
out for us.

Consequently, in any of the chapters following, we can only talk about genre in the most general way, always looking to specifics to help us thread our way carefully through the sophisticated and complex reality that underlies the blunt instrument of musical categorisation.

Simply, then, the categories we will be looking at will include the elements of style that are common to Blues, Jazz, Gospel, Country and Rock. No element is exclusive to any of these genres, and indeed, that is the problem for voice teachers at the beginning of the 21st century. 'Pop' itself has come to stand for a different listening experience altogether – it is the difference, perhaps, between Britney Spears and Mary J Blige. Pop is a massive fusion of all these early genres and it tends to re-present them in a 'lite' version.

But where do singers turn when they want to learn how to sing in any of these styles? Well, to themselves, by and large, because for many singing teachers, popular music or popular styles can't be 'taught'. There's nothing new in encountering these attitudes – indeed, this is an age-old debate in the arts that, though raised often enough, never gets solved. Can you teach theatre directors? Can you teach poets? Can you teach painters? Popular singing is largely defined by the singer's style, and can you teach style? The 'you've either got it or you haven't' school would say no – they would argue that the people who master their arts have a highly tuned sensibility which leads them to their own highly personal discoveries. Such people can be nurtured but not taught.

Some of these ideas are historically situated. Teaching in the arts is a relatively new idea, although the master–apprentice relationship has a long and respected history. New subject areas that are taught in formal situations (at academies, or institutes of higher education), however, must struggle for some time to attain a level of academic respectability. Consequently, when a new course in creative writing or theatre directing emerges, it takes much to convince people that there is something in it. The people who teach on these courses would probably *not* profess to believe that they can 'teach' someone how to write a fine poem or how to direct a brilliant *Hamlet*. They might however have absolute faith that the elements of a fine poem or a brilliant production of *Hamlet* could be analysed, discussed, and applied in varying combinations and situations. They might also have the temerity to believe that a student who might otherwise have spent years on their own making these discoveries could be led on a much more organised path to those same discoveries.

There have probably been relatively few voice teachers who believed that they could 'train' artistry – most will have thought that what they *could* do was to impart an extended knowledge of the elements of vocal artistry. How the singer puts those elements together has always been the result of the singer's particular selection and application. In most cases, voice teachers and their students today have much the same relationship as that shared a century or two ago between the pupil and the 'maestro'. It is not altogether a master–apprentice relationship, but neither is it usually a formally 'taught' subject.

This means that much of the student's experience depends upon that of their voice tutor.

Because the great majority of the work I have done as a trainer has been in *un*doing the work of a voice teacher, I have become increasingly aware of something that never occurred to me when I was a young performer looking for some vocal training: many voice tutors have no formal instruction in teaching voice. In fact, very few do. While that may sound worrisome at first, it must be remembered that in most art forms, teachers are teaching without having been taught *how* to teach in that art form. This is because most art-form teachers rely upon a combination of experience, practical knowledge and inspiration to guide students through to making their own discoveries. And in most cases, this works well – especially if the teacher has significant awareness of the various elements of that art form, an ability to articulate those elements clearly to a student, and a great amount of experience in the professional world that s/he can draw upon. While a great many voice teachers have such experience, the difficulty for the students with whom I often find myself working is that their experience is rarely in popular music.

Anyone who has ever tried to find a voice teacher with popular music experience will know the difficulty here, and it's partly one of educational structures. At an early age, students interested in or talented at music are generally ushered through the 'classical' music repertoire, and vocalists seem to go one of two ways. Either they decide to start their own band and experiment with popular styles (with greater or lesser success), or else they 'get serious' and learn to sight-read, join the choir or, when advanced, join a madrigal or acapella group. They may possibly go on to study Classical or Operatic repertoire. There is a limit to the number of people who can sustain a living in this world, but many people educated in this way do go on to become choir directors, musical directors and/or voice teachers. Pupils who go in this latter direction frequently have the ready skills to become voice teachers: they have a sound knowledge of classical music repertoire, often have adequate piano skills to accompany their students' lessons, and will have a knowledge of vocal technique that has been adequate for training in Classical repertoire for many centuries. When I was searching for some guidance 20 years ago in California, the teachers I encountered often 'allowed' work on a Musical Theatre song or two; however, the focus of their teaching generally remained on Classical repertoire. These days it is much more common for vocal teachers to work through Musical Theatre repertoire, although their approach often remains a solid extension of Classical technique.

The move from music student to voice teacher seems logical: the move from being a Rock singer to being a voice tutor doesn't. Consequently, if you go looking for a voice teacher, you can find plenty of good, talented people who can teach the fundamentals of vocal production, but whose popular repertoire extends only as far as Musical Theatre. This is a problem if your musical interests lie in the more popular music areas – in Rock or Jazz or mainstream Pop vocal style. Most voice training is a combination of explanation and demonstration, so most voice teachers will feel comfortable teaching the music/style of Stephen Sondheim, but not the music/style of Aretha Franklin. And in my time of teaching, I've learned just how many frustrated R&B soul divas there are out there!

A little personal history

My own journey as a vocalist may help to explain why I feel this book to be both necessary and – I hope – useful, since in my ensuing conversations with other vocalists, I've learned that my years of confusion were not unique. I spent most of my time as a professional singer wishing that I didn't have to view the instrument of my expression as such a mystery. I felt that there were times when I understood why I was singing well and times when I didn't. Sometimes I found myself making sounds I hadn't 'planned' to make, and while these were *not* always what I wanted, I was at times pleasantly surprised. I had days when I felt I could sing forever, and times (sometimes up to three months) when I felt my voice would never fully come back. Some days I could hit every note in my 'natural' range, and other days I was lucky to croak out a little over half. When I started, I knew that I seemed to have a huge, 'belting' lower end of the range, then about one and a half notes of squeaky noise, followed by a thin, reedy sound at the top end. I knew that I was fortunate in having a fair old range in the bottom end, since essentially that was all I brought to market. But over the years I learned that I could adjust the sounds slightly and suddenly have a kind of bright and powerful sound in that 'reedy' upper register, and could even 'hide' the squeaky noise by imitating sounds I had heard made by other singers. But I had no real understanding of how I was doing it.

When I began singing professionally (by which I mean someone actually *paid* me to do it) at the age of 15, I was lucky to have been starting at a time when there was a growth of 'coffee houses' along the California coast where even an underaged singer could find work (there was little or no alcohol sold in these venues). Of course, there wasn't much that was 'professional' about it, apart from the fact that the $5.00 a night I earned made it my first job. As vocal jobs go, it wasn't terribly demanding: I sang two sets a night, and on only three or four nights a week. There were times in these early days when I felt able to use the whole of my range – even that detested 'head voice' – and the relative lack of strain meant that after the first few weeks, I had little or no problem sustaining the vocal demands of the songs I was doing: a combination of traditional Folk, and what might be thought of as 'contemporary' Folk in the songs of writers like Leonard Cohen and Joni Mitchell.

Within a year, I had abandoned this vocal 'safe house' for the more demanding styles of Rock singing. My first bands were doing a range of original as well as cover versions, which made different demands on my voice; I quickly learned to categorise these and place them in the appropriate part of our sets: Motown sort of dance numbers (easy), Janis Joplin (hard), Aretha Franklin (sometimes impossible at the high end). Over the years I thought many times about going to see a voice teacher, just to see if I had the basics right. But apart from a few brief (and not very successful) encounters, I did not seek out voice training until some years after I'd stopped singing professionally.

In 1990 I was working at the Central School of Speech and Drama in London as head of the Acting programme. As an acting teacher I have always been acutely aware that the majority of the lessons I learnt as a professional actress came through singing – particularly in the exploration of text set to music. As I faced the prospect of updating and rethinking parts of the Central curriculum, I was determined to get more musicality into the teaching structure.

During my first two years at Central, we hired a number of external singing teachers both to teach and to direct projects. Whenever I watched them I was profoundly disturbed; at the end of each project I felt that if only I had the courage to do it, I could get a better sound out of the students. I had no training, apart from that outlined above, and I knew that I really had no vocabulary for teaching music. However, I decided, after watching a particularly disastrous musical revue, to ask the students if they would be willing to put some time into workshopping the material with me once again outside the curriculum. They were eager and helpful and we began simply by taking each piece in turn. As I watched, I attempted to create a language of working with them that they could understand. Slowly over the next year I added more singing teaching to my schedule and, while I still felt insecure and aware of my lack of formal training, I knew I was getting results.

In my third year at Central, I was informed that we would be starting a Musical Theatre course. This added yet another cohort of students, all of whom needed to have one-on-one tuition in singing. It was further decided, in light of my expanding role on the voice side, that I should take some staff development time and funds to bolster my technical voice skills. I began working with respected West End voice coach, Mary Hammond. Mary understood that I was seeing her largely to learn from her methods and to discuss with her the methods that I would be using with our new Musical Theatre students. She was extremely open and generous about her work, and I learned much from those lessons as her student – and even more by watching her work with others when she came to Central to run occasional workshops for us. I happily realised that in many ways, Mary and I were teaching the same fundamental things, but we were using a different language. Mary's, I felt, was far clearer to students from the outset.

As the course grew at Central, a new voice tutor, Gillyanne Kayes, joined the teaching staff. She spent half an hour a week with each student and it was obvious to me that she was getting terrific results. As I was still working with the voice students, I became increasingly concerned that students should not become confused between Gillyanne's classes and my own, so we began watching each other's work. I found myself to be increasingly fascinated with the way in which she was teaching.

Gillyanne explained to me that much of what I had been watching was based on an American method, pioneered by a woman named Jo Estill. As I grew increasingly interested in its directness and clarity, I began attending weekend seminars given by Gillyanne in Estill Voice Training Systems (EVTS). For the first time in my singing career, I found that I had a language that made some sense of my own voice. I also found that although the Estill method can be very complex, there are a number of simple things that students can learn quickly – and that these simple things can go a long way towards clearing up the confusion that attends some vocal training.

After leaving the Central School to take up a post as head of Acting for the Liverpool Institute for Performing Arts, it became clear to the head of the

Music department that finding someone to teach Rock and Pop vocal was going to be a problem. Given my background, I was the obvious choice for taking on such a challenge, but I was still feeling that technically I had much to learn. At Central the focus of my work had been in Musical Theatre, with only the occasional need to coach someone through a Rock or Pop ballad in preparation for an audition for shows like *Hair* or *Rent*. I knew that teaching vocalists who were seriously interested in studying Pop or Rock styles would demand even greater technical confidence on my part. As early as my first term I faced a student who had largely sung in school choirs and in Folk groups who wanted to know how to sound like Chaka Khan. Another wanted to hit the high notes in Aretha Franklin's *Ain't No Way*, but could only do so in her 'opera voice'. The more I searched, the more surprised I became at how little training was available to singers in this area. So, in order to provide a logical teaching pattern that would extend students' ability to approach a number of different styles and sounds, I began to compile notes on various stylistic approaches and to preside over some critical listening sessions with my second-year vocalists. This book is the extension of that process.

A few years ago I attended an EVTS course in London taught by Jo Estill herself, and I made a number of discoveries about the way in which varying elements of the Estill system can be used in teaching popular vocal style. Jo herself claims that the great strength of her method is that it can be used for any style of music – although, unsurprisingly, at the nightly sessions where students could get up and work a song through with Jo, the repertoire never strayed from Opera and Musical Theatre. This, I felt, wasn't because people weren't interested in popular styles. These days, voice teachers have to be able to train students who can sing in *We Will Rock You* or *Mamma Mia!* And as the West End seems increasingly bent on importing Rock musical styles, voice teachers will increasingly need to find methods for teaching that aren't derived from the old Classical schools. I think the reason we didn't cover these styles at Jo's coaching sessions was that most of the voice teachers attending came from the world of Classical music, or else the focus of their background was on more traditional Musical Theatre styles. For some, perhaps, there remained the old idea that Classical singing is 'good' singing.

Certainly the focus of any book I have found on singing remains pretty squarely on the 'bel' part of 'bel canto'[1]. Centuries of music produced by Western Classical composers have encouraged the trained voice always to

---

1 Bel canto translates as 'beautiful singing'. The term is used to describe techniques that originated with Italian singing masters and performers many centuries ago, and these days generally means approaching voice training within the parameters of Classical methods and aesthetics.

strive towards a perceived notion of an aesthetically beautiful sound, and even today most Classical voice critics operate within a pretty closely prescribed consensual aesthetic boundary. Popular singing, of course, is as often as not about disrupting those aesthetic prescriptions – when vocalists like Hank Williams or Bruce Springsteen sound wonderful to us, they may simultaneously sound anything but beautiful. The consequence of this is that the break from the 'beautiful' tradition is a difficult one for most voice teachers to negotiate, since the majority of the tools they work with are geared rather specifically to guiding voices towards that perceived aesthetic of good singing. To expect them to train popular voices, then, is rather like expecting an oil painter to sculpt – it requires different tools and an open mind towards a different kind of experience.

I once read an article by Thomas F Cleveland, director of Singing Arts and Sciences at the Vanderbilt Voice Centre in Nashville. I found it fascinating, because he seemed to be pleading with voice teachers everywhere to recognise that with the growth of popular music, they must learn how to teach popular styles. His brief article made the point that for too long, people have believed singing in the Classical style to be the only 'healthy' way to sing. I hadn't run across such a plea before in any published work, although in my professional life I had encountered many who were convinced that singers either sing 'properly' or risk ruining their voices completely. Professor Cleveland finished his article with an admonition: voice teachers would have to keep an open mind, and they would have to learn the science of what makes commercial styles what they are. I'm not sure there could ever be a *science* capable of accommodating just what it is about Bessie Smith's style that has such a sexual charge, or why Roy Orbison elicits such deep emotion when he sings; but I do believe there are a number of elements that can be taught, and that these will allow artists to explore the possibility of creating such effects in their own way, should they so choose.

My musical journey has led me – in what I freely admit to be a patchwork, uneven way – to some discoveries about teaching students the elements of style, and it is those elements which form the basis of this work. As a foundation, I still rely very much on things I've learned over the years from great teachers like Mary Hammond, Gillyanne Kayes and Jo Estill. But I know that when I was starting out as a teacher there were many times when I could have used some kind of reference or vocabulary for approaching popular style.

This is one good reason, I hope, for writing this book – the fact that so little is available in the way of either vocabulary or teaching tools for teachers or students in this area. However, there are other reasons for thinking that this analysis might be useful. The first is the big change over the last decade or two in Musical Theatre repertoire. For many voice teachers, the need to coach their pupils through auditions for Rock and Pop musicals has increasingly become a worry. The popularity of 'back catalogue' musicals, as well as the rising influence of young Musical Theatre composers (Jason Robert Brown comes to mind) whose styles are more 'pop' than traditional Musical Theatre style, has challenged many voice teachers – some of whom have no practical experience of working in more popular idioms. The second is the rapid growth of demand for teaching in this area – whether that demand is in the 'informal' sector (short-course or youth music areas), or in the growing number of popular music performance courses in the formal education context, so many of which carry singing as a component or pathway of the course.

Of course, outside the educational areas, the popularity of 'reality' shows such as *Pop Idol* and *Fame Academy* has meant that our interest in the styles and variety of popular voices and singing is increasingly apparent. And while the subject matter and the 'art' behind the expression in popular singing may be elusive and controversial, I hope that this book proves to be a helpful step in trying to identify and describe some tools for practice in this area. The many workshops and classes that I have done based on this material have suggested to me that it is.

In short, then, this book is *not* about training the voice – there are many resources for this, from classes to videos to one-to-one tuition. It aims instead to be an aid both to singers and to voice teachers who want to explore the ways in which they can add more style to their work, but are not sure where such an exploration might start. I very much hope that the following pages will inspire greater vocal experimentation in the quest to find unique and exciting sounds that can add to the singer's own expressive ability – indeed, this has been my mission throughout the writing of the book.

TEACHING AND LEARNING STYLE

To train or not to train?

> ... in order to become a professional performer you must master the science of vocal control. Only a vocal master has the knowledge and complete range of expression totally at his or her command that is necessary to communicate with the audience.
>
> Gloria Bennett – *Breaking Through*[1]

I'm trying to imagine a description of vocal aesthetics for the beginning of the 21st century, but it isn't easy. Such an idea would be ludicrous to contemplate in the world of contemporary art, and similarly the idea that there is a universally held understanding of what constitutes 'good' popular singing is too simplistic to accommodate the varieties of experience that we have with popular singers. It would be fairly safe, however, to say that such a description would not have been unthinkable 100 years ago. The 'bel canto' ideals of purity of tone, smooth and uninterrupted sound throughout the range, graceful note endings, pleasing width and speed of vibrato, direct accuracy in note

---

1 *Breaking Through* (2nd edition), Gloria Bennett (Milwaukee: Hal Leonard Corp.) 2001, p. 2

attack throughout even the most florid of passages – these would generally have been upheld by singing teachers for most of the last century. The useful thing about such an agreement over a desirable aesthetic in any art form is that it makes life easier for everyone involved. If we all know what 'good' art is, then we can certainly set about more easily identifying and 'correcting' that which is 'bad'.

To a great extent, voice teachers are still working with some fairly rigid ideas about what constitutes 'good' and 'bad' singing. 'Pleasant', 'smooth', 'accurate' and other such adjectives are still as common as ever, and probably always will be; but when measured against the reality of recorded popular song from the very earliest decades of the 20th century onwards, they seem almost completely inadequate criteria for judging the strength and effectiveness of a singer's performance. On and off throughout this century it has been common to describe some vocalists as 'song stylists'. To an extent, this may perhaps have been the ideal way to get around the difficulty we face when we acknowledge that some of the singers whose work has been most powerful and influential have been those whose approach was heavily 'stylised' (i.e. not necessarily beautiful or even pleasant!). What else could explain the top 100 list produced by Radio 2's 'Voices of the Century'[2] accommodating such diverse artists as Bob Dylan, Judy Garland, Paul Robeson, Tom Waits, Vera Lynn, Johnny Cash and Julie Andrews?

In preparation for this book, I spent some time researching to see if anything has been written about voice that could be useful to people with a practical interest in popular singing. I found a number of voice training books and systems for approaching popular singing, but was surprised at how often they base themselves on traditional ideas.

Some still seem to emanate from a notion of 'mastery' – an idea that I think is particularly difficult to apply to popular singing. I suppose if you asked many popular singing artists if they felt they had 'mastered' singing, they might simply be confused. That confusion would no doubt come from them wondering what exactly it was you were asking if they'd mastered. Gloria Bennett's idea, quoted at the top of this section (that one can only become a professional performer if one has mastered the science of vocal control), must only be applicable to Classical singers. There are hundreds of

2 'Voices of the Century' was a listeners' poll commissioned by the BBC in 2001. The top 10 artists in order were: Frank Sinatra, Elvis Presley, Nat King Cole, Ella Fitzgerald, Bing Crosby, John Lennon, Aretha Franklin, Billie Holiday, Barbra Streisand and Freddie Mercury. BBC Radio 2 is, of course, a popular music station so one would not have expected voices from the Classical world to feature in this list.

professional performers who are wholly untrained in their 'science' yet regularly communicate profoundly with their audiences. This doesn't mean that a singer might not find Bennett's training ideas useful – only that it surely cannot be right to assert that one can only become a professional performer if one has 'mastered vocal control'. Leonard Cohen or Curt Kobain became very successful professional performers, but it would be strange to describe such artists as 'masters of vocal control'.

After a brief spell of reading books on voice training for contemporary singing, I have been reminded of the kind of confusion I felt when I first heard singing teachers at work:

> The fundamental principle of the Italian school was that 'the beauty of the tone quality is the result of the freedom of tone production.' This principle is just as true for the heavy metal vocalist as it was for the great opera stars of the past.[3]

So who is determining what constitutes 'beauty of tone' here? And who listens to heavy metal singers hoping to hear 'beauty of tone'? Surely in order to consider styles as extreme as heavy metal, we can't get far by applying the principles of the old Italian singing masters. Heavy metal singers aren't after 'beauty of tone'; they're after creating a highly charged, visceral experience which convinces their listeners that what they're expressing is too deeply felt to be fashioned as an 'artistic' expression in that old Italian-school way.

Other books can be confusing because they carry such 'aesthetically loaded' instructions. Anne Peckham's *The Contemporary Singer* is a great book, full of very solid and traditional approaches to voice training that will, in her language, help you to avoid 'poor tone quality', 'harshness', or 'breathiness'. That's all well and good if you truly feel you want to avoid these things. But of course, these adjectives aren't always pejorative when it comes to creating style in popular music – and in some cases they can (and I would argue that they should!) serve descriptively without carrying the judgement they seem to bear in the context of so many books I've read about the voice.

After all, 'poor tone quality' depends to a great degree upon material and circumstance. I have been singing for a long time, and will admit to being pretty judgemental – yet I'm not sure that one can make easy judgements about tone quality in popular singers. Perhaps you could argue that com-

3 *Breaking Through*, Bennett, p. 21

paratively, singers like Robbie Williams or George Michael have 'good tone quality'. But I wouldn't want to hear Robbie Williams or George Michael sing *Tangled Up in Blue* or *I've Been Loving You Too Long* – they singularly lack the raw emotional power of artists like Dylan or Otis Redding. So I'm not sure that good tone quality is necessarily part of the right criteria for judging the artistry or the depth of a performance in popular music.

Does this mean that we shouldn't train voices for popular styles? It is certainly the case that the great majority of the vocal pioneers of Blues, Rock, Gospel, Country and Jazz were not trained singers. Many successful contemporary artists in these genres have not been trained – yet so much depends upon the individual voice. Most of the budding young style artists making musical noises of all kinds in bedrooms and garages across the land don't initially think of having voice lessons – they follow that other time-honoured route, imitating the 'masters' (or, if not 'masters', then at least the artists whom they feel inspired by at any particular time).

I happen to think that there are many good reasons to train voices – and perhaps that is the legacy of hearing my father's advice when I was young. He is an artist, and when I used to paint or draw as a child he would say: 'You have to learn the rules before you can break them effectively.' That made a lot of sense to me. But the truth is, I sang professionally for many years with no training and no 'rules', and while my later education in voice production was interesting, it obviously wasn't necessary in order to earn a good living as a singer for more than a decade. Some years ago I met another artist who had gone to art school and trained as a painter. He was forever experimenting and trying to defeat the 'logical' side of his brain that just couldn't forget 'the rules' for long enough to break them. He finally began painting with his left hand (he was right-handed) and found it wonderfully liberating.

So what is the answer? In the end, of course, it's an individual choice and if you do seek training, there are some helpful things to consider. The first, I think, is Richard Miller's assertion that 'one of the main goals of [singing] teaching in this and any age should be to do no harm'.[4] It may sound obvious, but it *is* important – especially in the area of popular singing. It is reasonable to assume that (as he is paraphrasing Hippocrates), Miller is referring to physical harm, because he follows this with a reference to 'healthy vocal function'. I would extend his worry about doing harm into the arena of the singer's psyche, since so much of my teaching seems to centre around trying

4   Richard Miller, *On the Art of Singing* (Oxford: Oxford University Press, 1996) p. 221

either to undo the strict aesthetic 'rules' of singing that teachers have inculcated in young voices (which although well intentioned, often result in dull or uninspired sounds and a fear of experimentation), or else in trying to encourage singers to consider what uses may be made of their vocal idiosyncrasies (which are usually seen and described as faults or flaws by traditional voice teachers).

It is no doubt this concern with sustainability that has inspired so many voice specialists to write books like those referred to above. The need to inspire young artists to think about creating a healthy and sustainable sound is an important one. Vocal technique (of whatever kind) must be sustainable: indeed, in the absence of anything absolute in aesthetic terms, perhaps sustainability is the most important thing for popular singers to consider. And even though this sounds straightforward and relatively uncontentious, there will still be many who would insist that Tina Turner or Tom Waits sing in 'unsustainable' styles. For many other voices, these sounds *are* unsustainable, yet Tina Turner and Tom Waits are still going strong after many decades of performing. This means that sustainability must be measured against the individual voice and its capabilities.

The unique sort of 'constricted' or rather 'damaged' sound that some singers produce may be the result either of something unusual in the vocal anatomy itself, which results in a scratchy or rough phonation, or else the result of some vocal damage. But the real question is: would their many devoted listeners want these vocal flaws 'fixed'? Probably not – but neither would voice teachers be working responsibly if they *encouraged* vocal damage. And herein lies much of the difficulty in teaching popular style. It is undeniable that many artists work 'without a net' in popular singing. When the aim is gritty vocal realism, then 'pleasing tone' and 'flawless technique' are not important. That may be heresy to voice teachers, but it is undeniably the case for many popular singers.

This means that if you decide to work with a voice teacher, you should keep in mind that you need to find someone with whom you can communicate really well; who will be sympathetic with your desires to explore the styles you're interested in; and who can keep an open mind about the kinds of noises you might want to make. *Most of all, that person should be able to help you determine how best to guarantee vocal health and sustainability.* While it may be fine to work at all those things which traditional voice teachers concentrate on – beauty of tone, breathing, bridging the 'break' in the voice artfully, etc. – you must remember *as* you work on them that these things belong to a certain set of beliefs (that tone should be beautiful; that breaks need to be bridged or smoothed out). And you also need to remember that this set of beliefs doesn't apply to Björk or to Little Richard. One of my hopes in writing this book is that it may prove a useful starting point for both students and voice teachers in the process of building a vocabulary of style and sound that can help when exploring vocal expression through popular styles.

Singers who decide *not* to work with a voice teacher must keep in mind that they alone will have to serve as the monitor of their own vocal health, and take seriously the responsibility for its well-being. Whatever your current musical passions, remember that life is long! Addionally, you want to be adaptable enough to suit your voice to the kind of styles you may be passionate about 20 years from now. Rod Stewart began with *Maggie May* but these days he's singing Cole Porter. Longevity and sustainability should be your aims, and if you reach any point at which you feel uncertain about anything you're doing vocally, you should seek professional advice.

Cultivating vocal style

Most popular music allows the singer an extraordinary freedom. Indeed, this is the thing that both seduces and frightens many vocalists. There are some great advantages to that freedom – often the singer can freely improvise, changing notes and note values as they go along. To a confident singer, this can be a wonderful challenge; to the singer used to reading just what's written on the sheet, it can be extremely intimidating. Most musicians know the difference between working with players who have only a limited knowledge of music theory but can improvise freely, and working with players who have been 'reading the dots' all their lives. Most musicians, I would wager, value those players who can do both.

For vocalists who have spent many of their formative years singing in choirs and Musical Theatre, the thought of singing in a Rock or Jazz style often creates some insecurities. So what is it about vocal style that we can learn in order to approach it with some confidence?

As noted in the Introduction, defining style is a difficult thing. It could be considered, when talking about a singer's style, as a personal 'signature' in the execution of a work, or perhaps as a collection of definitive traits detectable throughout a range of works. But however you look at it, style is almost certainly a derivation from and a reaction to both the music and the world that the artist is exposed to. We often use the term 'style' when we're talking about musical genre – such as Rock-style or Jazz-style singing. For singers who want to think seriously about their own style, and who wish to find ways in which to broaden or to adapt their own style successfully to different kinds of music, it is necessary to look at both uses of the word *style*.

Many young singers I've worked with (particularly those with an interest or background in Rock music) seem to feel a kind of resentment towards the idea of thinking too consciously about their singing style. They point to the more extreme examples of vocal style (Randy Blythe from Lamb of God, or Joe Cocker come to mind) and insist that style is something that should grow 'instinctively' and may wilt under the light of too much scrutiny. Like most young artists, Rock vocalists can often feel that their own style – insofar as they may be able to describe or understand it – has evolved as a sort of 'happy accident' and they're reluctant to tinker with it too much. There's much to be said for such a theory, and I'm not at all against the 'happy accident' mode of vocal exploration. But as most singers' careers go on, it isn't uncommon to find that some stylistic vocal choices can begin to feel limiting. All artists need to keep changing and growing, and since the voice and its own 'natural' properties (such as range and tone throughout varying qualities) can often feel like a rather stubborn thing to change, style is a pretty amenable place to start the evolutionary process.

Not all vocalists, of course, have the option of finding and holding doggedly to their own style in the rough and tumble of the entertainment business these days, so increasingly I find myself encouraging even my most die-hard young style geniuses to contemplate the fact that vocal adaptability can often mean more employment options. I can think of one ex-student whose strong natural Rhythm & Blues style was both wonderful and limiting. She could find occasional gigs with bands, and sometimes worked with a local Gospel group, but her hard work in classes gradually allowed her to successfully adapt her Rhythm & Blues instincts to other styles, so that at the moment she is happily working in the West End – and she knows that she is only at the beginning of her career. Her options are greater now, and that gives her more confidence in her ability to keep working.

Of course, not all stylistic choices are or should be made on the basis of flexibility in the market, but I think it is important to note that some are. Whatever else it is, or however we may want to go about obtaining it, vocal style is always a personal statement of some sort about one's take on the world, whether traditional, progressive or rebel/anarchist. And this is where there can often be sensitivity around the idea of teaching style. Just as one would have to think hard about how to approach teaching someone else how to 'dress better' or 'dress differently', I always keep in mind the delicacy needed in talking to voice students about how to explore style. Nearly every student I encounter possesses some kind of innate style with which they feel comfortable. I always think that if I'm doing my work well, that innate, comfortable style will simply grow and become more flexible, more creative, and offer the student more pleasure in singing. In truth, it is relatively rare for me to encounter a student who isn't at least interested in exploring another style – often it's simply that they don't know where to begin, beyond trying to imitate a few bars in the style of Joni Mitchell or Frank Sinatra. While that is not a bad place at all to start (and I usually make sure that every student I work with has done a similar extended exercise), the student often doesn't know how to proceed from there.

As we'll explore in later chapters, this almost always depends upon where the student wants to go. When I'm listening to a student for the first time, I can often detect what their musical influences have been. These days, the sphere of that influence seems to be narrowing. When I first started singing, I was aware that other vocalists and musicians I knew were usually familiar with a range of popular vocalists and styles. But lately the students I encounter have generally listened to 'chart' shows for most of their lives and been exposed, roughly, only to whatever has been on *Top of the Pops* for the last eight or so years. That has an effect on their sound, just as my more eclectic tastes have always influenced the style choices I make. When I sing, it's easy, I think, to detect my love of Rhythm & Blues and Gospel – particularly in such voices as Chaka Khan's and Aretha Franklin's – but perhaps what distinguishes (or confuses!) my sound from theirs is an equal admiration for the vulnerable expressions of Judy Garland, Ethel Waters, and Hank Williams. Whatever you learn in listening to a particular singer's style, it is certain that that style has derived from or is reacting to specific sources. Most singers know this to be true to a large extent, although style, like any other part of human expression, is subject to unconscious impulses. Consequently, I will not be the only vocalist who has been surprised over and over again at what listeners 'swear' they have heard in my singing style.

In my capacity as an acting teacher and director, I find myself speaking to actors about approaching style in a different way. For the actor, this area can create some pretty strange confusions and lead to some uncomfortable artificiality. The best tend to approach style as a question of what is rewarded in a given sphere or society. To discover a truthful way of playing in styles as diverse as Restoration or Russian naturalism, the actor needs to examine what particular things (for example, in expression, dress or behaviour) were 'rewarded' within the social context of these characters. Despite the different approaches required by these disciplines, the actor's lesson is sometimes applicable to the vocalist's, but works in slightly different ways. Often singers will recreate the kind of sounds that they have been rewarded for in past performances, which can occasionally result in them feeling stuck with the sound they've been validated for. External factors can also have an effect – many singers either consciously or unconsciously adopt the sounds they hear in successful vocalists, even if these sounds don't fit particularly comfortably into their own voice. The consequence can be that singers find themselves choosing vocal habits that are not always beneficial, or else don't seem to come naturally from the singer.

For example, a few years ago I encountered a student whose voice was extraordinarily loud. When I first heard her sing we were in a small studio and the sheer volume she could produce was overwhelming. As I listened to her first end-of-term showing pieces, I could imagine that for much of her life, that extremely loud quality had been what her audiences or fellow musicians had noticed most about her voice. Many vocalists I know would love to be able to produce even three-quarters of the volume that this young woman is capable of, yet over time I became aware not only of some increasing huskiness in the sound she was producing, but also of the limits that volume was placing on her ability to make different, subtler or more flexible vocal choices – which, in turn, was limiting her ability to find a range of expressive vocal choices. We spent a year looking at a number of different options in terms of onsets, sustain, decay, improv, effort-level, and emotional connection in her performances, and listening to artists she had never really examined before. We chose artists whose emotional power wasn't connected to size or volume (like Peggy Lee and Chet Baker). Her dedication paid off in so many ways: she finished her second year with a showing that surprised many in terms of the nuance and delicacy she was able to bring to the same kind of music she was singing so loudly a year before. Her voice lost the huskiness that was worrisome in her first year, and she seemed able to find a much deeper pleasure in her singing, because her choices were so much greater.

In that same year, I encountered a young woman who had listened for so long to the fluttery, high, melismatic sounds that distinguish singers like Mariah Carey and Christina Aguilera, that she found herself feeling that she was only 'really' singing when she was *over*singing. All music – from R&B

ballads to show tunes – were processed through the 'mill' of her vocal acrobatics. The result, for her, was that she often heard criticism about her singing because it sounded rather 'robotic'. When we began working she told me that she wasn't sure any more what her own style was and had no idea where to start looking. We spent our year listening to artists she'd never liked before – concentrating on those who sing tunes simply, with little or no improvisation and few vocal decorations. We chose some 'beautiful' voices (KD Lang) and some 'homely' voices (Leonard Cohen). What the student realised was that she'd spent many years thinking that singing all around the melody was synonymous with expression. She discovered that finding her true expressive ability within a melody and lyric as written was a great liberation. Her end-of-year showing was astonishing to many, who found the simple, connected honesty of her work rather breathtaking.

Some people think that learning the craft of singing popular music in this way results in a singer with no style of their own – but I believe that nothing could be further from the truth. Many fine artists begin their study with copies of the masters, and yet very few of them become 'stuck' in the style or process of another. They learn and they synthesise. They copy and then they adapt. The process of finding individual style is always a process of successful selection. The more there is to choose from, the more there is to discard.

For all these reasons, cultivating style can often mean significantly broadening what you are listening to. It is true that most people have some strong immediate reactions to certain styles of music, but I find that once you spend the time really listening to what a vocalist is doing and what kind of stylistic choices they're making, you can come to appreciate even the kinds of music/singing you thought you didn't like. Keeping an open mind and exploring widely is really important in developing your style: so is trying out genres and sounds that feel foreign to you. Although doing so may feel at first like trying on a suit that doesn't fit, the objective in such exercises needs to focus firmly on seeing how you can use sounds/vocal choices you don't habitually make to express your own ideas about a song, and to communicate those ideas as effectively as possible. If you work in this way, you may very well find that it isn't that the 'suit' doesn't fit – it's just the not the style you usually wear.

Why is Pop/American Idol *often so dull?*
Perhaps nothing more clearly demonstrates the difference between genre and style than reality shows like *Pop Idol* or *American Idol*. There's never any doubt, once you get right down to the last contestants, that what you are watching

are singers who understand genre. They know how to perform a Rhythm & Blues song, a Pop song, a Rock song or a Country song. In the final rounds the voices are usually really impressive in terms of tone, pitch and range. And of course, the competitive element of these shows can be gripping (after all, 40 million viewers can't be wrong). But there is far less to interest an audience in terms of style. That's because style – of whatever kind, from fashion to interior design to fine art – is always a question of revealing something about yourself. Singing isn't the only expressive media through which we can often be shy or tentative about honestly revealing ourselves; for most people, such open revelations are rare and we save them for particular moments, with particular people. We are more likely to expose our real thoughts and feelings when writing, for example, or when engaged in another solitary activity.

The problem with approaching style in a public way – which is something that great singing artists have to do – is that it carries with it a kind of 'double bind'. Most singers want their audiences to like what they're doing. But the moment we become too concerned with pleasing others (the difficulty for the *Pop Idol* contestant!), we risk obscuring the very things about ourselves that are singular and interesting. Think of those moments when you're really trying to impress: at job interviews, or meeting your partner's parents for the first time. The natural thing for most people to do in such situations is to become bland or 'pleasant'. It could well be that what really makes you remarkable is your razor-sharp wit and ready laughter, but instead, you tend to tone everything down – *especially* your razor-sharp wit and ready laughter. There are of course some people who refuse to adjust their personalities to their situations. We may think them foolhardy or stubborn, while admiring their courage in remaining true to their own identities.

If we think about this in terms of singing, we realise that what most singers are looking for is the best way to express honestly what it is that makes them unique. But pursuing this can require some bravery on the part of the artist. It must have taken some courage for singers like Big Mama Thornton, Howlin' Wolf or Janis Joplin to sing with such abandon and so little concern for the usual aesthetic considerations of what makes up a pleasing sound. And that courage paid off in terms of their audience's appreciation for the raw, direct and honest sounds they made.

This is what makes teaching vocal style both challenging and interesting. The most important thing in exploring style is, of course, to do so with no regard to pleasing anyone. And even though I regularly plead with students to stop listening to their own voices and start thinking much more about communicating – in raw, unusual or even ugly sounds – what it is they feel, they often find this very hard. I've also learned in doing this kind of work that if you have a really great voice, it's going to work both for and against you. Sometimes it will be capable of producing a pure, gorgeous tone that pierces the heart just at the right moment. And sometimes you get so addicted to your own beautiful sounds that you create lovely musical wallpaper and communicate with no one but yourself. If you have a poor or limited voice, you will probably come to style work with some frustration but with more initial openness. You may be frustrated with your lack of range or perhaps a less-than-beautiful tone – but if you concentrate your efforts on communicating what it is that makes you *you*, you'll quickly learn to enjoy the incredible range of sounds that any human voice can produce.

What style is it?

Does it matter? There will have been a time, perhaps 20 years ago or more, when all this was simpler. Most record stores I frequented as a teenager had five major sections: Classical, Rock, Country, Easy Listening, and Jazz. True, it was easy to confuse some artists – say Frank Sinatra, who was sometimes found in Jazz, but usually in Easy Listening. But most of us were growing up at a time when broadcasting meant *broad*casting, so we watched the Ed Sullivan show and others like it, knowing that there would be something for everyone – Frankie Laine *and* the Beach Boys; Edie Gorme *and* the Beatles. Musical exposure was a bit more mixed in those days, but nevertheless the categories seemed clearer to me and, of course, there wasn't so much recorded music. Today the categories seem to be growing every time I walk into HMV or surf the Amazon.com website, and I get dizzy with the proliferation of new sub-categories. Just under 'Pop' on the Amazon site I have to make a choice between: Brit Pop, Dance Pop, Adult Contemporary, Doo Wop, Latin Pop, Easy Listening, Motown, Nostalgia, Singer-Songwriter, Soft Rock, Traditional Pop, Vocal Pop. I can think of seven categories to put Billy Joel in, and even more for Stevie Wonder. Even the 'Large Category' section has expanded on the 'big five' of my youth to cover Blues, Gospel & Christian, Classical, Country, Dance, Folk, International, Jazz, Miscellaneous, Opera & Vocal, Pop, Rock, Rap & Hip-Hop, and Rhythm & Blues/Soul. At least there are fewer crossover possibilities here, and that makes the whole process of trying to define 'style' a bit easier.

When I began thinking about putting my teaching methods into some kind of order, both for my students and for myself, I considered organising the information into these kinds of categories. However, in our discussions we found that the categories were too limiting, so we decided instead to try choosing artists whose style we felt epitomised certain categories. We didn't get very far: the whole method fell apart once we got around to considering individual artists, since so many of the ones we discussed seemed to be 'uncategorisable'. In the end, I simply broke down what I felt I had learned, in the three decades I had been either singing or teaching singing, about the elements that comprise different styles of popular music. In considering each of these elements we then looked at how they were – or were not – employed by singers across a range of styles, and set about mastering those that we could and experimenting by applying them in a variety of songs.

It seems logical, then, to present them in the same way in this book. We will start with the weightiest elements (vocal qualities), and then follow these with the complementary elements (those that shape and modify the sound). We'll also look at how various artists put these elements together and what the effect of such combinations are.

But it also seems logical to look at the differences in popular genres – Blues, Jazz, Rock, Country, Pop – even though everyone knows that *there are no hard and fast rules*. One could argue all day about whether Billie Holiday is a Jazz singer or a Blues singer. I would say the former, but I see her work classified as Blues all the time. Many singers cross over the lines all the time, and that can make it harder to put them into a category. The point of working with genre categories is *not* to make rigid distinctions, but to see whether or not there are some kinds of common characteristics that might help us in our journey to explore various vocal styles. For this reason, the next section of my book is set out in categories that attempt to distil some basic, common characteristics that one can find in vocalists who fall (loosely!) into Jazz, Blues, Country, Gospel, Rock or Pop genres. For those students who wish to find a facility in one or more of these popular genres, or for those students who have to find a Jazz song for a specific audition, I find that these very basic 'common characteristics' can be helpful in figuring out how to get started when working on a particular type of popular singing. **However, I always recognise that there are no real categories, and that musical evolutions and fusions will always defy any attempt to put things into rigid boxes.**

Sound, mystery, panic

Some of the sounds outlined below and described over the next chapters aren't particularly pleasant in and of themselves. Some of them border on what many voice teachers consider to be bad or even dangerous. Most voice teachers will tell you that constriction of any kind is bad/unhealthy/ dangerous for a singer, and by and large I wouldn't argue with that. But I also know that popular singers do it all the time, especially Blues and Rock singers, and I've come to believe that when we talk about bad/unhealthy/ dangerous, we need also to realise that generalisations about the voice are always that – generalisations.

Particular voices can have particular qualities and capacities, and this is an area of vocal work that desperately needs more research. It's very difficult to understand why some voices can sustain so much more hard usage than others. It's also difficult to know why – when the voice is being produced in a clear, unconstricted way – some vocalists seem to have unfailing endurance while others must keep a careful watch over the length of time they are singing for or the strength/volume of sound they are producing.

One of the first Rock bands I worked in had three lead singers – an expensive but interesting option. One of my fellow lead singers was a young man named Roland who was passionate about Rod Stewart's raspy vocal quality. Roland was convinced that Rod had damaged his voice through hard living, and that this damage was responsible for the wonderfully husky tone quality in *Maggie May* (he believed this track to be the greatest Rock recording of all time). In the summer of 1970, Roland set out on his one-man journey towards vocal disaster. Every night after our gigs, which didn't generally finish until 2.00 a.m., Roland took himself off to the shores of Huntington Beach and there, with a bottle of Southern Comfort (preferred tipple of the raspy Janis Joplin), he would drink and sing at the top of his lungs for hours in a quest for vocal calluses. It was a fine plan – sandy, but promising. He usually sang until he fell asleep. Occasionally one of us would accompany him but it wasn't, to be honest, all that fascinating to watch.

Roland stayed with it for most of July and August, but despite his best efforts, the results were disappointing. Worse than that, he found that his voice was stronger than ever and his one-time tendency to go hoarse on long nights or when he pushed notes particularly hard seemed to vanish completely. His voice remained disappointingly clear and certainly stronger, and I can still remember the suppressed laugh and the assumed solemnity all around the rehearsal room when Roland bitterly announced the failure of his nightly howling to the ocean.

What can we learn from this? To be honest, I'm not sure. Roland was young, his voice was obviously strong – perhaps the warmth and moisture of the Pacific Ocean air in a Southern California high summer was a tonic of some sort? Perhaps Southern Comfort has some little-dreamt-of qualities? Maybe there was just something peculiarly strong in Roland's vocal constitution that could accommodate this kind of 'abuse'. I couldn't begin to explain it. But I do know that general rules about voices have their limits. And I feel convinced that if Roland had gone to any singing teacher to describe his plan, the teacher's reaction would no doubt have been panic. I am also convinced that if Roland had described the plan as one by which he intended to strengthen his vocal endurance (which is what, in the end, he achieved), a singing teacher would first have laughed and *then* have panicked.

In my own case, I knew that the amount of singing I was doing was staggering. Apart from performing five sets, six nights a week, we often put in four or five hours of practice sessions up to four times a week. I was singing extremely demanding Rock repertoire – some original, some cover versions – and I used to worry at times whether I would do some long-term damage to my voice. I worried about the long term, because I could rarely ever see a problem in the short term. The times when I *did* lose my voice were nearly always the result of one of two things: viral illnesses, or time off. The first seemed understandable to me; the second, mysterious. Most years, after the New Year, we would take a week or two off. When you're working as a musician there's no such thing as paid holiday, so time off is a rare thing. And as much as I looked forward to it, I always dreaded the inevitable vocal problems it would entail once we started up again. Inevitably, the first month after a two-week lay-off would be filled with difficulties – rearranging sets and material to cover the hoarseness and the temporarily limited range of my voice.

These days, I wouldn't generally advise a student to keep singing, 40 to 50 hours a week, that many weeks out of the year, if they wish to maintain their vocal health. But for me, that was the recipe. I can't explain it any more than I can explain Roland's 'ocean therapy'.

Human voices make surprising noises all the time. I've heard noises made by indigenous Folk singers that sound very unhealthy, yet the singers making them have been going strong for years. I've heard babies that can Twang and Belt for hours, even when I've thought they couldn't possibly go on without getting hoarse. I often try to imagine what most singing teachers would say to these babies, or to the gurgling, rasping 'overtone' Folk singers of Eastern Europe. But then again, I often try to imagine what they would say to Louis

Armstrong. My point is that there comes a time when teachers have to realise that vocalists with experience probably know the capacity of their own voices better than anyone else.

In this book, I encourage people to make some strange noises. As a teacher I've always tried to entice people away from the sounds they feel safest with, and to open their minds to the possible beauty in the 'unbeautiful' sound. I realise that in doing this, I am courting some criticism from traditional circles. I also realise that a singing teacher will often work with a student who has no control over how many hours they must sing. And for many singers that's often the greatest hazard to vocal health – not trying to imitate Tori Amos or Tom Jones, but trying to keep the voice going for eight shows a week. In these situations, singing teachers *must* keep the student aware of the safest and healthiest vocal choices available. But when a singer is *not* in this difficult position, I think there's little need to panic about experimenting with sounds of all kinds – and in allowing the singer to find out for themselves just what their voice can and can't cope with.

I have been singing and teaching singers for nearly 30 years and I still think there's much to be said for respecting the mystery of the voice. Not only the mystery that surrounds each individual voice in terms of sound, ability, endurance, etc., but also the mystery inherent in our inability to understand everything about its workings. There's great mystery in why we react so strongly to the sound of the human voice in the first place, and much to baffle us in varieties of reception to the varieties of sung sounds. I've learned that the voice is somehow so deeply entwined in the way we perceive and project our identity, that changes in the sounds we make can elicit some extraordinarily surprising emotional releases that can't be explained. I've lost count of the times that I've coached young women who have been making quiet, breathy sounds into finding their own strong natural sound – and who have cried almost uncontrollably upon first hearing it.

And like most people, I've found myself unable to suppress my own unexpected emotional reaction to sung music – whether that has come as a sudden outburst of tears while listening to a Gospel choir in South Africa, or as a sense of overpowering spirituality that literally stopped me in my tracks while hearing a Russian Orthodox quartet at the Alexander Nevsky Monastery in St Petersburg. In its older sense, the word 'mystery' was often used to connote both an individual craft (as in the Medieval Mystery guilds), and also in contemplation of the spiritual. I would like to think that the mystery I refer to here could be applied successfully in either sense.

A PRACTICAL GUIDE FOR EXPLORING YOUR OWN VOICE

The basic singing skills

Before we begin, we need to consider what is fundamental to singing in *any* style. One of the great distinctions between teaching 'classical' singing and popular singing is that popular song has evolved out of years of free experimentation with sound and style. This means that the range of choices for popular song production is greater than the range for those you might hear in the Cardiff Singer of the World competition. For Classical artists, the training is incredibly demanding, and the vocal skill necessary is daunting to most of us. For popular singing, as we know, neither of these is necessary. It takes a generous heart to think of Johnny Cash as a skilled singer, and no one imagines for a moment that Bob Dylan had much training. But popular music is an enormous category and most people know that a voice like Whitney Houston's is both very skilled and has probably had the benefit of some training.

Despite the relatively forgiving nature of popular music when it comes to technical skill, there are still some bottom-line skills that are truly helpful in enhancing a singer's ability. And despite the importance of these skills, the bad news is that there is relatively little known about how they work – and even less known about how to help the singer who doesn't possess them!

The first of these is the need for any singer, popular or Classical, to pitch notes with accuracy. The tone can be like a gravel-mixer (Tom Waits or Leonard Cohen), or as piercing as that of a screaming cat (Kate Bush or Björk); improvisational ability may be negligible and the delivery rather artless (Carole King or Suzanne Vega); and even the overall audibility/comprehensibility can be completely obscured (Rickie Lee Jones or Chet Baker) … but whether or not the voice is technically exact, a singer needs a pretty reliable ear. There are some exceptions to this, and nearly every studio engineer I've ever known has endless tales of how they managed to save some recording from the woeful pitching of some artist or other. But if a reliable ear is an important quality, sadly, there isn't much remedy available to help poor pitch, and I've never found any quick cures.

Any number of people have proposed possible solutions to pitch problems, and many singing teachers will insist that there *is* no 'tone deafness' – just a lack of confidence and familiarity, or problems of one sort or another in vocal production. While any or all of this may be true, there is still very little of a practical nature that has ever been produced to truly help someone 'build' reliability into their pitching. While there are some good theories, there is still little evidence to suggest that anyone understands exactly how we improve pitch in all cases. And certainly, the more I read, the more contradictory is the advice I'm given.

Many people warn of the difficulty of learning pitch from hearing notes on a piano, yet I know of one singer who, after years of being told that he had a lovely tone but flawed pitch, decided to take some action. He spent more than a year practising daily with a piano and a tape recorder, matching the sound on the keyboard with his own and listening to the playback. He found that for the first time he could hear the pitch problem (but only when playing sounds back on the tape recorder) – which was an important first step towards correcting it. He kept at it with amazing perseverance, and found that by the end of the year he was being asked to do much more lead vocal in his band. He didn't stop there, but carried on recording and listening for another year. He was 21 when he sat down with the piano and the cassette recorder – he has now been singing solo professionally for more than a decade.

His story may be exceptional (there is much need for research in this area), or it may be that anyone with his dedication could achieve what he did. I'm certain that what he was actually doing was not 'improving his ear' so much as learning to *feel* the pitch instead of relying solely on *hearing* the pitch. He was convinced that hearing the note wasn't the issue – he had realised this when he listened back to the sounds he'd made when trying to accurately reproduce a note he had played on the piano. While he could hear the difference in pitch in this playback, he could not hear the difference when he tried to match the note 'live'. In any case, I do tell my students that I have seen someone 'fix' their pitch problem and that it *may* be possible for anyone to do so. But I never leave out the hard truth about the length of time it may take.

I have also learned that pitching is closely connected to confidence and overall health. I have seen many singers 'lose' their ability for a time, only to rediscover it as they persevere. As with so many things about the voice, focusing too exclusively on any one area, like inaccurate pitching (even though this is a *fundamental* problem), can exacerbate the difficulty – by causing tension or creating a loss of confidence in the singer. I've recently worked with a young woman from Norway whose pitch was causing some distress both to herself and to the music staff. In our first semester of working together we spoke about the pitch problems and she said that she could hear them but felt baffled because she'd never had pitch problems before. As the semester went on I was baffled as well, since for at least 95% of the time she was pitching correctly. In the second semester I decided that perhaps refocusing attention might help, so I assigned *The Midnight Sun* as her assessment song. *The Midnight Sun* is a difficult song for many to master, as the melody is a complex series of descending chromatic lines, and I was hoping that by concentrating on *melody* rather than *pitch* (a subtle distinction) we might get somewhere. We did. In all our sessions, I asked her simply to keep the overall structure of the melody in her head, rather than to concentrate too closely on whether she was pitching it accurately. We discussed the pattern of the melody, and what made it so unique and challenging, and at one point I asked her to draw the melody as a continuous line. And in her assessed performance, she managed to pitch the melody perfectly. I include this story here not because it clears up the mystery of pitching – in fact, if anything, it may confuse it further; but it is perhaps an illustration of how the language and the imagery we use in teaching and learning can be important. By making the problem one about the pattern of a beautiful melody, instead of one about pitch accuracy, this student managed to conquer it.

The second skill is neither as difficult for most, nor is it as crucial as the first. It is the ability to produce or control vibrato. This is not as necessary to creating good performance as accurate pitch, but without it, a singer *may* feel themselves to be limited. Vibrato is at once one of the greatest assets and one of the greatest mysteries of the singing voice. I have never encountered any singing teacher (or indeed method) able to adequately explain what it is, or how (or even *if*) you can teach a singer to access or control it – although many singers can naturally do these things without any difficulty. I have seen laryngoscopic[1] films of the voice while producing vibrato, and the only visible evidence of it is that there is a detectable movement or 'shake' of the whole of the laryngeal structure. If you have vibrato, you should be able to feel this movement simply by wrapping your hand very lightly around the front of your throat and observing the mild 'shaking' of the larynx during its production.   .

Some singers say that they sense their vibrato coming from the area of their throats; some say they feel it in their chest; and others swear that the sensation comes from their stomach. Some can control the speed and/or the width of their vibrato, and this control allows a far greater stylistic flexibility. Many singers notice their vibrato growing more pronounced as they grow older, and some, particularly singers aged over 60, can feel a tendency in the vibrato to 'wobble' very widely, producing an unpleasant sound that nearly falls out of the range of pitch.

Some people have no control whatsoever over their vibrato. If the vibrato is relatively even in terms of speed and width, this isn't a great problem. If it's very fast, it can lead to some great frustration for the singer, but doesn't rule out the possibility of producing some interesting pop sounds (think of Randy Crawford!). I have worked fairly successfully with singers in getting the speed of the vibrato to slow, and often that work has included a focus on anchoring the head and neck muscles to restrain the 'shake' of the vibrato a bit – although I've also seen that same anchoring work make the vibrato *more* pronounced. Like pitch, vibrato difficulties often grow stronger under the light of scrutiny and sometimes it's best simply to keep working towards relaxation in order to enable the vocalist to get in touch with whatever muscles are involved in the production of the vibrato. For many singers, vibrato is a strong muscular memory of their vocal production being teamed with a particular speed or width of vibrato.

Along with the problem of too much vibrato, there are many singers who are equally frustrated at the complete *lack* of it in their voices. Some voice

---

1 Laryngoscopy is a diagnostic procedure that can be done in a few ways, but the method most common for singers is performed with fibre-optic cable which has a tiny camera. The flexible cable is threaded through the nose and down into the throat so that the practitioner can see the larynx directly.

teachers believe that this lack of vibrato is common in young voices, and that with enough practice the singer can slowly learn to add vibrato to the sound. I have worked with students who said they had no vibrato or could not imagine how to access it, and who then surprised both themselves and me by suddenly hearing a bit of vibrato while they were singing. This may be because for many singers, vibrato only occurs when they are fairly relaxed or confident in production. It takes a while to feel this way when you're singing in front of someone, so perhaps when a singer does manage that, the vibrato occurs naturally. Often, when we're concerned about accuracy in pitching or about making a beautiful tone, we create so much tension that we simply stiffen all our vocal 'works' to the extent that the gentle laryngeal shake I described earlier can't take place. Certainly if you can sometimes suppress vibrato by adding a bit of muscle anchoring, the reverse should be true. In any case, I would say that it's best to 'discover' vibrato by not concentrating on it too much – you may just bring on enough tension through that concentration to suppress it! What the singer must remember is that while a lack of vibrato may be frustrating in some styles, in popular music there are a great many very successful singers who rarely ever use it (and as you'll see in the interview with Paul McCartney, there are some artists who actively dislike the whole idea of vibrato).

All of the above leads me to the conclusion that there is still much research to be done on vibrato. I have seen teachers mistakenly explain to their students that it is a function of pitch oscillation, so that in order to create vibrato they should try moving rapidly between pitch variations. Any singer with vibrato knows that this isn't true: in most vibrato, there is a variation of the pulse that determines how we hear the 'pitching' element. In other words, vibrato that sounds 'right' to our ears tends to be within the range of 5–8 pulsations per second. Pulsations slower than 5 per second are those which we tend to hear as straying away from the pitch. Those faster than 8 per second are generally described as a tremolo and can sound strange, but do not tend to threaten the pitch.[2] The best a singer can do in practising these quick pitch oscillations is learn to produce a good vocal 'trill', but the sensation of moving quickly between two semi-tones simply isn't the same as the sensation most feel when producing a 'natural' vibrato sound, and doesn't have the same pulsation. But some voice teachers feel that learning to create this 'artificial' vibrato will encourage the creation, ultimately, of a 'natural' one.

2 Meribeth Bunch, *Dynamics of the Singing Voice*, 2nd edition (Wein, New York: Springer-Verlag, 1993), p. 75

In the end, it appears to me that pitch and vibrato have much to do with each other, since pitching in itself is not an exact science when it comes to the human voice – indeed, the more you know about it, the more confusing it can seem. In her analysis of the acoustic variables involved in pitching, Meribeth Bunch examines the work of F Winckel, who asks 'is a certain inaccuracy in intonation actually necessary for satisfying auditory impression?'[3] – and while the many variations that arise in perception studies on pitch and vibrato suggest that this may be so, she still concludes that these variations 'do not relieve the singer of the responsibility of producing correct pitches and of being "in tune"'. Perhaps. But we need to remember that some styles can tolerate more variety in the category of 'in tune' than others. And we also need to remember that confidence plays a *major* part in these areas. All this means that if you're serious about improving your sound, you need to sing as often as you can, and you need to enjoy the sound you make – yes, even with all of its 'flaws'! You must also be patient about your progress. Sometimes voices change slowly, but they do change and they do grow, all the more so as you work on and enjoy them.

Some key concepts

Most voice-training systems concentrate on three basic areas: the source of power (this is what actually 'drives' the sound – breath and lungs); the source of sound (anatomically, the point at which sound is created – contained within the larynx); and sound manipulation (anatomically, the controllable 'follow-on' areas which we use for modifying the sound – the pharynx, or vocal tract, resonators in nose and mouth, muscles all around the neck, jaw and the face, lips, etc.).

The source of power

In my teaching, I don't expend much energy in discussing breath as the power source of the voice, or worrying overmuch about breathing. In my experience, worrying too much about 'correct' breathing can sometimes create tension. Most voice students and tutors know that inadequate breath capacity can be a problem: sometimes this is the result of something medical – asthma, bronchitis, and other ailments of the respiratory system can all affect breath capacity in either the short or the long term. These are not areas

---

3 Meribeth Bunch, *Dynamics of the Singing Voice*, 2nd edition (Wein, New York: Springer-Verlag, 1993), p. 75

for a voice teacher to be 'guessing' in, so they always require professional medical advice. Some students clearly have more capacity than others, and while there are exercises that can, perhaps over time, allow some expansion, change is usually very slow.

When I have talked to students about breathing, it's often been a way of getting them to contact muscles that can help support a large sound. In other words, instructions of the kind I used to hear endlessly (breathe into your diaphragm or – more interestingly – into your stomach or pelvis) are both good imagery and bad anatomy. There's only one place in the body into which we can draw air. But we *can* use different muscles when we breathe. Whether you move the muscles around your lower torso, or the muscles around your shoulders when you breathe, you're still inhaling air into the same place – into little sacs in the lungs, where the bronchial tubes widen to complete the exchange of oxygen and carbon dioxide. Breathing deeply can require you to contract muscles which must then move to make way for greater expansion of the lungs; it doesn't literally mean that you're 'breathing into your stomach'. When I talk to students about breathing, then, it's often a way of getting them simply to contact and move the muscles they will need for producing big sounds.

PRACTICE

You can quickly get in touch with a lot of the muscles you need for singing – and particularly for making big, powerful sounds – by using the breath. Lie down on the floor and make sure you're comfortable (you might want to keep your knees bent). As you breathe, allow the air intake to move various parts of your body:

1. Breathe 'into' your collarbones and your shoulders. This is often the most common part of our bodies that we 'breathe into'. You'll notice that it's a fairly shallow breath and won't support you long under any stress or strain.

2. Now place your hands over your ribcage. When you breathe in, use that breath to make your hands rise or move gently outwards. Be aware of the muscles that move underneath your hands.

3. Next, place your hands on your stomach and use an intake of breath to make your hands move upwards. Again, be aware of the muscles that move underneath your hands.

4. Finally, try to use the image of breathing 'into your back'. You should feel some different muscles expanding and pushing down into the floor.

This is not meant to be an anatomy lesson. However, using the image of 'breathing into' various parts of your body is a good way to identify the larger muscles that can help to support you in the work of singing. When we're working really hard (and make no mistake – many varieties of singing require very hard muscle work!), right at the upper end of our range, or using a lot of volume, we need to be aware of 'anchoring' that sound by engaging all the muscles we've just felt working. It wasn't only heavy-metal theatrics that used to inspire hard Rock singers to swing their microphone stands around. The old mic stands used to have quite heavily weighted bases – and swinging the stand upside down while singing the big notes helped more than one hard-rocker to engage all the muscles needed to produce sounds of size and passion.

Perhaps the greatest reason why I don't like discussing breathing when teaching singers is that I have all too often experienced (either in myself or in others) the tension that this can sometimes create. There isn't a great mystery to breathing. We do it all the time – even if we are often doing it in rather shallow ways. We generally know instinctively how much breath we need to take to get to the end of a very long sentence, and, when speaking, we are rarely caught out needing more breath unless we have developed a habitual laziness about our 'tidal' intake. But because we aren't planning the lyrical pattern in a song in quite the same way as we plan our own day-to-day conversation, getting through a lyrical line can sometimes require that we breathe differently. Any number of singers have come to me with sheet music marked by some vocal tutor with little 'x's telling the student where to breathe. It's pretty hard to approach a song this technically and still make it live within your imagination. For the most part, I believe it to be a big mistake to divorce technique from imagination. At some point, you'll have to put the two together in performance, and you will inevitably find that process difficult if you've not been doing it from the beginning.

Of course, many songs from Classical or 'legit' repertoire specifically challenge the singer's ability to get through it all with brilliant breath control (some Gilbert and Sullivan 'patter' songs come to mind, as do some Sondheim numbers), but the great majority of popular song can work if you 'breathe with your thoughts'. In other words, find out first what the thought pattern of the song is – where your thoughts or actions are beginning and ending, or where you go on to a new thought – and then *speak* the lyrics. You'll know exactly where to breathe. For the most part, that's where you should breathe when singing the song, too.

Because breath is often a source of anxiety or closely associated with a state of anxiety, concentration on breathing can too often lead to mild hyperventilation and tension. Concentration on breathing can lead to 'over-breathing' – in other words, the singer takes in far more breath than needed, and then either blasts the air out at the beginning of the phrase or creates tension somewhere as they strive to release air as evenly as possible. Forget it. Unless you are training in Classical repertoire, or have a very specific problem with capacity, or find yourself cast in one of those Gilbert and Sullivan roles, try to breathe with your thoughts. Try also to remember the lower torso area muscles we contacted in the breathing exercise above – stay in touch with those stomach, back and ribcage muscles and try never to raise your shoulders when breathing. If you can manage that you should be fine!

The source of the sound

We'll be working a lot on this throughout our practical exploration of the elements of style, but let's start with a little anatomical understanding. The larynx itself is often the biggest mystery to the singer, as its workings are totally hidden. There are parts you can feel – you can pretty easily feel the thyroid cartilage which houses the vocal mechanisms, and with practice you can find a way to sense when you're manipulating true and false vocal folds.

There are a number of things it may help you to know about laryngeal anatomy, but I'm going to cover only the things I feel you'll *need* to know in order to make sense of the rest of this book – so stay with it, and I'll try to be as brief as possible.

The larynx that you're feeling when you touch the sides of your throat looks like this:

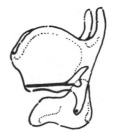

Figure 1 Side view of the larynx

This is a diagram of the vocal folds – as if you were looking down on the vocal mechanism:

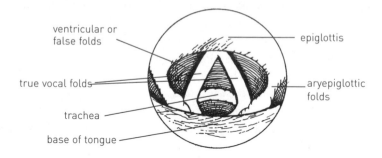

Figure 2 View of larynx, inhaling, showing the vocal folds

The true vocal folds are connected in front to the thyroid cartilage, and attached at the back to two small pieces of cartilage, called the arytnoids. The movements of these small arytnoids determine the length and the width of the folds when the vocal process is operating. Just above the true folds are the false folds – something I never knew I had before studying Jo Estill's system. No other voice teacher I had come across explained the importance of learning to manipulate the false folds – and particularly the importance of learning to keep them 'retracted' if you want to produce a clear, unconstricted sound. The false folds are protection: they protect the delicate vocal mechanism, and they work in an emergency to protect the whole of the respiratory system.

PRACTICE

If you want to feel the sensation of these false folds closing quickly, grunt as hard as you can. That 'strangulated' sensation is the feeling of the false folds closing quickly. If they close while you're trying to produce tone, you can usually hear that your sound becomes 'constricted'; it has the same sort of strangulated property as the sound you made when you were grunting. Now get ready to make that grunting sound again, but this time see what happens if you sing a note while holding all that tension.

Something pretty strange (it could be terrible or it could be wonderful – depends upon your point of view!) will probably emerge. This is because when the false folds constrict over the true folds, they interfere with the free and natural vibrations that produce tone. Think of what happens when you place a piece of paper over a tuning fork – you still hear tone, and you know that the tuning fork is still vibrating, but there's a buzzing sound that interferes with the free, natural sound of the vibration.

Because the true folds are a more delicate mechanism than a tuning fork, prolonged interference from the false folds can, over time, cause damage. The health of your vocal folds depends upon their ability to vibrate unhampered.

As the false folds are the source of so much anxiety for singers, it's worth taking a moment here to try and get a feel for their working.

PRACTICE

We've looked at how to make the false folds constrict by making a grunting sound. Do that again; this time, try to hold onto that feeling. If you've got it, try sustaining the sound of a grunt and then releasing it quickly. At this point the false folds will have opened back, but they will not be as widely retracted as they could be. For that to happen, try laughing as hard as you can – silently. Make it a real 'ho-ho-ho' kind of laugh and notice that you feel a very 'wide' sensation in the area of your larynx. Try to hold onto that feeling. Breathe in and out a few times, and you should notice that your breathing is absolutely silent. In fact, breathing as audibly as you can and then consciously silencing your breath over four or five really deep inhalations is another quick way to feel that retracted sensation.

The true folds are open when you're inhaling, and they seem 'close' when you begin to make sound. In fact, they are vibrating at incredible speeds (262 times per second to pitch a middle C), so unless you have a slow-motion film, they look as if they are closed in a larygoscopic picture. They relax and open again when you take another breath. When you're singing loudly, the mass of these folds is generally thicker and they close in the vibration for longer. When you sing softly, the mass of the folds is thinner, and folds meet for a shorter fraction of time in the vibration. Once we progress to looking at the various voice qualities, you'll see that the length and density of the folds themselves have a big effect on the actual sounds that you're making, and learning to change these variables is a part of expanding your possibilities as a singer.

Learning to keep those false folds retracted is an important skill that can help you to keep that 'constricted' sound out of your vocal production – unless, of course, you want to use it. This is an idea that is anathema to most vocal teachers, but we can't look at the elements of popular singing without admitting that there are many singers – particularly in the Blues and Rock genres – who employ constricted sounds at various times in their singing. This is another area that needs some careful research. I have worked with many singers who can produce a mildly constricted sound for a fairly prolonged time, apparently without damaging their vocal folds. Equally, I have worked with those for whom even a short spell of trying to sing in this mildly constricted way causes an immediate sensation of dryness and needing to cough. There may be good physiological reasons why one voice can produce such a sound and another can't, but I have not been able to discover any research on the subject. Still, in my work I have learned that the brief use of mild constriction can be mastered by many, and can be extremely useful in raising the perceived level of effort that is demanded by some styles – for example, there is use for controlled constriction in some Rock and Gospel singing onsets. We'll look at these ideas in the next chapter.

Getting into sound

We're about to start an exploration of the sounds that you make, so it would be wise to do a little warm-up! One of the best ways to warm up is also one of the most common amongst voice teachers – it's called sirening.

PRACTICE

Sing the word 'sing' on a very comfortable note. Hold the 'ing' part of the word and very gently move up and down through the comfortable parts of your range. This exercise is called the siren because you'll sound like a very quiet siren when doing it. Be careful not to release the kind of closed sensation you have when you're holding the 'ing' sound. If you want to test the security of that 'ing' sound, release the tone very quickly into a 'ga' sound, and then move quickly back into the 'ing'. You'll quickly feel what muscles you need to hold that 'ing' securely in place. Keeping the back of the tongue nice and high (and the overall volume low) will help keep your siren in place. You will notice that this warm-up exercise doesn't produce much volume. It does, however, warm you up gently and if done for a few minutes will get you ready for some singing.

The larynx itself is a moveable mechanism and you will find that it naturally moves up and down as you work through your range. If you want to test that, place your fingers lightly against the sides of your larynx and sing from mid-range to your highest note and then down to your lowest. You'll feel this 'housing' mechanism moving up and then down. There are some vocal qualities in which the mechanism stays down a little longer, but it will inevitably rise as you reach the top of your range. The larynx is also capable of 'tilting', and it is this 'tilting' quality that gives your voice its musical sound. In other words, when you are speaking, your larynx generally remains in a neutral state; sometimes, when you are singing, it tilts slightly.

PRACTICE

If you want to feel this tilt, place your fingers lightly on the front of your throat. First speak a sentence: you will feel the mechanism staying more or less in place. Next, make the sound of a puppy gently whimpering. You should feel a slight pressure against your fingers as the larynx tilts forwards. Now try singing – it's best to choose something towards the top of your range, since some people use their 'speech' quality in mid-range, which means that the larynx stays pretty much in the neutral position. You should again feel a gentle pressure against your fingers as the thyroid cartilage tilts down and forwards.[4] There is another part of the larynx that tilts (the cricoid cartilage) when the voice is doing certain things, such as belting, but this isn't easy to feel.

---

4 Although this exercise will usually allow most people to feel this 'tilting', don't worry if you can't. I've lost count of the number of people in my workshops who swear they can't feel a thing, although they can always feel the tilt by placing their hands against my throat when I demonstrate. It must be that the larynx tilt is a more subtle process for some than for others.

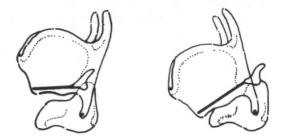

Figure 3 Side view of the larynx 'tilting'

The drawings above illustrate what's actually happening to the larynx when you do the 'tilting' exercise.

Exploring voice qualities

This is the part of the book where we start to make some serious noise! Take a bit of time with these exercises, and practise – perhaps where no one will hear you, as you'll no doubt be making some awkward noises at first, and you don't want to feel inhibited as you do so. I want to present the most useful and easily absorbed concepts in producing different vocal qualities, but I am aware that some people will require more detailed information or instruction (again, refer to the Resources section at the end of the book). Not all people who pick up a book like this want to teach or even to do more than expand their listening skills, so I will attempt to provide as balanced an overview as possible, always knowing that since each person's needs are different, my overview may be too simple or too complex for some.

The idea of working through different voice qualities is a relatively new one, but it has grown greatly in practice amongst voice teachers who aren't teaching exclusively in the areas of Opera or Classical technique. I think that Jo Estill's research has been instrumental in this growth of interest, and many teachers have expanded and modified her work in this area. Simply, the idea of training through different voice qualities is rather revolutionary. Traditional voice training systems see the voice as something emanating from one particular mode of production, which moves from a lower (sometimes called 'chest') register to an upper register (sometimes called 'head voice'), with a break or 'passagio' in between. By breaking down our analysis of vocal sound into various qualities, we can see the voice as capable of moving through that same range, but producing distinctly different kinds of sounds throughout.

This sometimes has the effect of helping to ease or solve the break or 'passagio' area (assuming that you *want* to — many popular singers never concern themselves with this), or even to alleviate the sense of a break in the voice altogether, depending upon the individual voice.

Various voice qualities have different vocal 'set-ups'. We'll learn these through simple access techniques as we go through each quality below. It is necessary, when both teaching and learning, to try to separate these qualities into their 'pure' forms (or as pure as possible), but the singer's art usually involves a skilful mixing of the qualities to achieve just the right sound for the right moment. In this section we will concentrate on producing the qualities in their raw state — so skill in 'mixing' and artistry will have to come later, when you've had a bit of practice!

As you go through the following exercises to help you try and access the respective qualities, *don't be discouraged if you can't get it right away*. Some people find it quite difficult to master more than a couple, especially at the start. If you find it easy to get all of them, you're one of those lucky people who possess a very flexible instrument. For the rest of us, repeated listening to artists who *do* use these qualities, together with lots of private experimentation (remember, you may not sound pleasant!), should slowly help you on your way. I've included CD examples of each of the qualities — *but because every voice is different, the sounds will vary*. Try to access the sound by following the steps and then checking again the section that outlines what you should have noticed when trying the sound. The CD example should be the last step — it's important to try it out for yourself first.

The common or neutral qualities

Quite a lot of popular music is sung in what I call the common or neutral thin-fold and thick-fold qualities. Some people think of these qualities in simpler terms — like 'head' voice or 'chest' voice — but I find these terms less helpful when teaching. For me, explaining to students about the variable density or thickness of the vocal mass helps to create an understanding of the ways in which we naturally mix qualities all the time, rather than always simply 'jumping' from chest to head. Let's start, then, by considering vocal-fold density. It sounds complex — but it isn't.

In anatomical terms, vocal folds can produce sound in varying degrees of thickness. Look at this side view of the larynx:

You'll see that when the thyroid cartilage of the
larynx tilts forwards, the vocal folds are stretched thin.
When the larynx is in neutral position, the folds are
thicker. There is a third tilt, which occurs when the
cricoid cartilage drops or tilts: this causes the back
end of the cricoid to push up and compress the folds
into an even thicker mass.

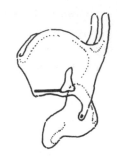

To understand why singing with a thicker fold
mass can be tiring, you could try thinking of the
difference between beating two bricks together and beating two pillows
together. Obviously because the pillows have less mass, they aren't likely to
damage each other, even if you beat them together very fast. Whereas, if you
had the strength, you could certainly manage to make the bricks damage
each other if you beat them together even for a short period of time. That,
in essence, is how you might think of the differences in vocal fold mass –
thicker mass naturally means more long-term wear and tear on the folds,
whereas thinner mass is a safer bet. Still – you wouldn't want to build your
house out of pillows. There's a time and place for all vocal quality uses; the
smart singer simply knows how to pick them.

THIN-FOLD

The first common quality is probably the one with which we sing Christmas
carols, or perhaps the one we use when we're singing lightly as we do the
housework, or drive in our cars (I haven't encountered many who use
extreme voice qualities such as Opera when driving in their cars, although
I'm sure they're out there). Many singers make a career out of using very little
more than this kind of common quality – Sade springs to mind, as does
Madonna in many of her songs. It's the quality that places, usually, very
little strain on our voices; we're probably expending most of our energy
vacuuming or driving (or dancing I suppose, if you're Madonna) when we
use it. At times it is louder than at others – in fact, it can sometimes be
remarkably bright and strong at the top end – which means the singer is
usually mixing something else (like Twang) into the quality. But even in its
relatively higher-volume state, it is rarely hard to sustain. This quality is
produced with thin vocal folds, and for most people it remains one used only
for the comfortable upper range. When we get to the too-high end or the
too-low end, we sometimes switch spontaneously to a different quality –
possibly Belt or Twang (which we'll look at below).

Thin-fold is a light, easy quality that has limited use in live performance such as Musical Theatre — although as sound technology grows more sophisticated, it is likely that Musical Theatre singers will find increasing use for this lighter, more 'natural' sound. Thin-fold is of greatest use in the recording studio where, mixed with other elements of style, it brings us close to the artist through its intimate sound. Many singers work in their comfortable, thin-fold range when beginning a song, and for most this is rarely the area of delivery that they want to develop, since it tends to come easily.

PRACTICE

Just to make sure you're able to feel what I'm talking about when referring to common thin-fold quality, it is worth trying a practical exercise to access and identify this sound.

1. Start at the top of your comfortable range and once again make the noise of a puppy whimpering. You should be able to feel your larynx tilt gently forwards.

2. Now slowly change the whimper into an 'ah' sound. Keep the sound light and try consciously *not* to engage muscles as you do this.

3. Get a real feel for exactly what's going on in terms of effort (which should remain pretty low/relaxed throughout) and sound (which should be relatively quiet) — and try to maintain it all the way through this exercise. Also be aware of keeping the larynx in its forward, tilted position.

4. Now very slowly move down through your range, holding on to the same effort and sound/volume levels. Once you get near the bottom of the range you might feel like increasing either muscle or volume, or else releasing the larynx tilt — but hold on to your set-up if you can.

5. Try a little phrase from a song and, again, hang on to your vocal set-up and keep the effort and volume relatively low. You'll need breath for this, but don't overbreathe: just keep everything very

light and relaxed. You should aim to have the same feeling when singing the notes in your upper register as you do when singing the notes in your lower register. The overall sound will be a quiet but pleasing one.

Overall, this quality should feel like what you may think of as your 'head' or 'falsetto' voice. The point in trying out this exercise is to demonstrate that we can hold onto this thin-fold set-up for quite a lot of our range. How far it can be carried into the middle or low range will vary with each individual voice. The larynx naturally rises as pitch rises, and this results in the vocal folds being stretched thinner. Often as the pitch lowers into our mid- to low range, we feel the larynx going into a 'neutral' or untilted state. This makes the vocal folds denser. So this exercise is to help us hold onto that thinner fold mass for as long as it is comfortable.

THICK-FOLD

There is another quality common to popular singing that is rather like the neutral 'thin-fold' sound, in that it is one which many singers use with ease. It can sound, tonally, a bit like our speaking voice, but it is produced in a much more musical, 'sung' way. Often, if a singer has natural vibrato, it will appear easily in this quality. It is a sound that has greater power and potential for more volume than thin-fold quality, yet, like thin-fold, it is of most use in the singer's most comfortable range. Again, once the singer goes into the very high or very low areas of their range, s/he will often spontaneously switch to another quality.

You may simply think of this as your 'chest' voice, and, when singing in this thick-fold quality, you may or may not feel the larynx tilt. Because the sound is rich and strong, it seems certain that the mass of the vocal folds is thick. It doesn't require the same amount of effort that Belting does, and it doesn't feel as hard on the voice in production. It is often a very smooth quality and there are any number of singers who have made a career largely though the exploitation of this quality almost exclusively. Again, because these neutral qualities are ones that many singers find easy (natural?) to access and use, they rarely feel the need to work on them technically – although some grow frustrated by the limits of their upper range in the neutral thick-fold quality, and wish they didn't have to sacrifice its power by switching over into their neutral thin-fold sound.

In the simplest terms, neutral or common thick-fold is the singing sound you make when you are using a relatively moderate effort level, and singing in your low- to mid-range (where the folds will naturally be in thicker mass). Some people have great power in this quality, which can almost make the singer sound as if they are Belting; but this common thick-fold quality doesn't require the same kind of muscle or effort-level that Belting does.

PRACTICE

1. In what feels like the very middle of your range, try out the vowels A, E, I and O. Do your best to give the start of the sound an 'edge'. This is known as a glottal onset (which we'll work on again later).

2. While still in this mid-range area, sing A-E-I-O on one continuous breath – but use the 'edge' of the start of the sound to really distinguish between the vowels.
   a. Move up or down a pitch and hang onto that 'edge' to make the different vowels stand out from each other. Stay on one continuous breath, but you can hold onto each vowel longer now. Monitor what it feels like in terms of effort-level and volume. This will be a louder sound than thin-fold, but in mid-range it shouldn't really take too much more muscle than thin-fold. Once you've really got a full memory of the feeling and the sound, hang on to both and sing a phrase from any song (staying in your mid-range).
   b. The sound probably feels more 'saturated' – full and pure and right 'on' the breath.
   c. Move as comfortably as you can through the range – but don't push at the upper end. In other words do *not* 'drive' this quality by trying to engage more muscle or air in order to reach higher notes.

Doing these two practice exercises is a useful way of demonstrating that terms like 'head' and 'chest' voice aren't that helpful – even though it's true that people generally sing in thick-fold in their 'chest' voice and in thin-fold in their 'head' voice. But it's important to note that most people can sing in either thin- or thick-fold throughout quite a substantial part of their range.

Every singer will mix these qualities in that middle area where they often experience a 'break' in the voice.

These neutral qualities should just feel like a natural extension of the sounds you usually make in your life – but they are slightly sweeter, since they are sustained through your singing. In both of these qualities, you are often tilting your larynx forwards gently, so you will notice that this gives you – even in your easiest mid-range thick-fold sound – a slightly sweeter or perhaps warmer sound than your speaking voice.

Aspirate quality

In voice-quality terms, this is the only quality in which the vocal-fold mass actually stiffens slightly when you make the sound. The results can be a strange, airy tone, and many students cannot, at first, imagine where or how they would use such a quality. Actually, once they begin the serious work of really listening to the elements of style used by a given singer, they are nearly always surprised by how much Aspirate quality is used in popular singing.

PRACTICE

This is another relatively easy quality to access. First, imagine that you are doing that trick of blowing over an empty bottle to produce the weird, hollow sound that resonates up from the cavity of the bottle. If that makes sense to you, you've probably just mastered the onset for falsetto quality. If it doesn't, try the following:

1. Set your mouth in the position to say 'ooh'.

2. Instead of actually voicing the 'ooh', keep your mouth in that position and exhale audibly (you'll sound like the wind).

3. Next, voice the 'ooh'.

4. Now, try to combine the two – in other words, voice the 'ooh', *and* sound like the wind.

5. With this sound in place, try moving gently through the mid- to upper range.

6. Finally, hold onto the 'voice and wind' sensation and try singing 'Happy Birthday'.

You should have noticed the following:

1. When you made the sound, you could sense how much air was escaping freely as you did it.

2. If you put your hand in front of your mouth as you simply voiced the 'ooh' (step 3), and kept it there when you added the wind sound, you could feel the difference in production. The simple voiced 'ooh' shouldn't have produced much more sensation on your hand than a slight warmth. The aspirate 'ooh' should have produced a strong sensation of air hitting your hand. If this difference wasn't apparent, try again!

3. As you moved through the range, you may have found yourself losing the strong sensation of air on your hand – which may mean you switched into another quality.

4. You may have noticed that you didn't produce much in the way of vibrato. If you did, you may have switched into another quality.

5. When you sang 'Happy Birthday' you probably sounded as if you were doing an imitation of Marilyn Monroe (a pretty famous example of Aspirate singing, in fact).

6. Listen to CD example 2 and see if you think your quality sounds similar

---

Most students feel that if they produce this quality for very long, they become light-headed, thirsty or vocally rather 'tired'. They're probably not really tired, just unused to making this kind of sound – although they probably *are* light-headed and 'dry'. The amount of air escaping can make you feel as if the throat is drying out quickly. The exercise above (and the CD example) is done with Aspirate quality *at its most extreme* – most singers use it with far less air escaping. In fact, you might want to go back a practice, varying the amount of air you allow to escape while you sing. If you can keep the air present but somewhat minimal, you'll be able to employ this quality frequently without feeling dry or lightheaded. It's an extremely quiet quality and one best used in combination with other qualities.

Although Aspirate quality is not naturally loud, some singers using it can produce more volume than others. It is not, however, the quality anyone would choose for power. While getting the hang of it isn't difficult, learning to use it artfully can take some time. Often students will claim that this is exactly the kind of sound they want to *avoid* making, but, like other qualities, it all depends on where and how you use it. In the 'access' exercise outlined above, you're using a lot of air to make the quality distinguishable to you; as you get used to finding and using it, you can decrease that amount of air and still gain the benefits that Aspirate quality, or even a momentary stiffening of the vocal folds, can bring to song interpretation – particularly in terms of creating intimate or vulnerable vocal sounds. Few singers would use it too much, but singers like Norah Jones and Smokey Robinson have found terrific use for the Aspirate quality.

Elongated quality

No point in hiding it – we're getting into more unusual territory here. This quality took me much more time to appreciate, since I never 'naturally' used it in my years as a professional singer. However, having taken the time to understand it a little better, I now find it useful for all sorts of things – most particularly in getting a darker, more 'profound' resonance into the sound sometimes – and it seems to be a quality that I can use relatively easily over the *passagio*, or 'break' area in my voice. I find it easy to access in the lower end of my voice (where a lot of popular singers use this sound), but it can take a bit of practice to hold onto the sound as you move up in the register.

PRACTICE

Some people find this sound easy to access if they think about trying to make the sound of an adult crying in a low, mournful way. It can be particularly helpful to think of 'swallowing back' the sound as you make it, since Elongated quality is a muted, soft and dark tone. If you can imagine and produce the sound of an adult very mournfully crying as they say 'Oh, no', you're probably well on the way to mastering this quality. If you're not too sure, try the following:

1. Assume the imaginary state of exaggerated sadness – think of tragic films you've seen.

2. Place your fingers lightly against your throat.

3. Imagine a lot of space at the back of your throat. Don't compress the tongue down at the back to achieve this – think more in terms of gently 'lifting' the top of the back of your throat. If you've got this part right you should feel your larynx tilting slightly forwards.

4. Now, holding on to that physical state and the emotional sense of tragic loss, 'sink' into the sound of saying 'Oh, no'.

5. Try this a few times and then hold onto the 'o' at the end of 'Oh, no'; sustain it, as if singing instead of speaking. Keep the sound soft.

6. Once you've got the sustain, try moving up and down through a *very* limited low to mid-range – only three or four notes to start with.

You should have noticed the following:

1. Before you voiced the 'Oh' of 'Oh, no', you felt your larynx tilt forwards slightly.

2. In those few notes, the larynx didn't move.

3. If you tried to go up in the range, the larynx position began to feel a bit strained – this is because to make this sound, the larynx must stay in a low position. You can lower the larynx at any time, but because it has to rise when pitch rises, you need to *reach* the higher notes before you lower the larynx again. You can practise this by sirening up to a high note – not the very top of your range – and then (fingers lightly against your throat) trying to lengthen the vocal tract to drop the larynx again. This takes some practice, although most students can find this sound easily enough if they simply make the 'aahhh' sound that we sometimes make when we're finishing a yawn. This sound often starts high and comes

down in pitch and it's usually in perfect Elongated quality. So if the access 'key' above doesn't work, try making that end-of-yawn sound – it's usually failproof.

4. Listen to CD example 3 and see if you think your quality sounds similar.

Again, in its 'raw' state, the Elongated quality can make students wonder where they would use this eerie sound, although from the beginning they usually recognise that it has an interesting resonance. And while it isn't a sound that a singer can use to create much volume or power, it is a quality that adds a richness and uniqueness to many voices. As with the other qualities, its use as a stylistic choice can be wonderful when employed by the artist. It is just this quality, coupled with a tremendous gift for improvisation, that brings such pleasure in listening to singers like Donny Hathaway or Oleta Adams, who use a throaty sound to great effect.

Twang quality

Because this quality is so useful to popular singing, it's probably the most important of all to master, so we'll spend some time on it. In my work, I've determined that Twang has many subtle gradations. I often talk to students about 'hard' Twang, or 'baby' Twang. In our consensual way, we usually experiment and try out sounds so that we understand in the sessions what we're talking about. That's more difficult when trying to write out a 'prescription' or guide to making a sound. First let's try to understand the sound.

PRACTICE

Many people can access the 'hard' Twang sound by thinking of the noise young children make in a playground when they are teasing each other: 'nyeh-nyeh-nyeh-nyeh-nyeh'. If you know what I'm talking about and you can do that little taunting chant with a *really nasty* reliance on the nasal sound encouraged by the 'ny' combination ... well, you're probably a natural 'twanger'. It won't be a pleasant sound, so don't try to 'clean it up' or make it sound 'good'. Make sure you keep the vowel sound just as written above – 'eh'. If you can't find it this way, try the following:

1. Start with a good, fairly strong 'ee' sound in your comfortable mid-range. Imagine, as you are making the sound, that you are slowly 'compressing' it and pushing it out of your nose. It may help to 'squeeze' your face a bit as you do this. Now listen to CD example 4 and imitate.

2. Some people can access Twang quality by doing an American accent – but you might want to be sure you don't carry the accent into the song (unless, of course, you *want* to!).

3. For a 'baby' Twang, try to imitate the sound of an angry baby, crying 'wah' with a really nasal sensation. You may want to try to 'bend' the pitch upwards as you're doing it, just as the baby probably would. Listen to CD example 5 and imitate.

4. If you're having difficulty with these, try out the sounds of animals – either a sheep 'baa-ing' or a horse 'neigh-ing' – these tend to be 'baby' Twang sounds – or try the sound of a happy witch cackling.

For most people, one of these 'access' keys works. Once you have it, you should notice the following:

1. The back of your tongue will be very high – the sides of the back will probably be just touching your back molars.

2. The place where you really feel the sound is very high at the back of your mouth and in the nose.

3. The sound is very sharp, probably loud (although not always), and very 'brassy'.

4. The lower you are in the range, the 'harder' the Twang sound, and the higher you go, the more like a baby you sound.

5. Sometimes the two types of Twang ('hard' and 'baby') sound exactly alike when you listen, but should *feel* different when you are actually producing them.

6. In its pure state (as on the CD), Twang always sounds pretty unpleasant – sharp and nasal.

Twang sound is created when a small round muscle (the aryepiglottic sphincter) located above the folds is 'tightened'. A good way of understanding this, without getting too technical, is to think of what happens to the air in a balloon if, as you release it, you suddenly pull the little ring of the opening very tight – it makes a higher-pitched sort of squealing sound. In a sense, that's how the aryepiglottic sphincter works – it tightens and creates a brighter sound.

One of the reasons that Twang quality is so useful to popular singers is that it can enhance thin-fold quality. This is a surprise to most people, because they don't expect a thin-fold quality to have such power and volume. It is possible, however, for some people to have a very twangy Belt, and they can often begin at the lower end of the range with thick folds. If they don't adjust as they move up in their range, they can find the quality very stressful. For those who access this sound through the 'nyeh-nyeh' method, they will often produce that thick-fold Belt sound at first.

If you notice that you're finding it difficult to move up into your high range in Twang, re-think your mental image – I tell students either to remember the 'baby wail' described above, or to think of how they sound when they take a breath from a helium balloon. Make sure you don't force the sound at this point. Either of these images often sends them into thin-fold, 'baby' Twang easily. If you feel you can't adjust as you're moving up in your range, try starting off the Twang with the 'baby wail' sound or the animal sounds – they tend to start as thin-fold. The thin-fold quality of Twang is what makes it so useful for the Pop/Rock singer – you can produce enormous power and range in this quality which can be sustained for greater periods of time.

If you're finding it hard to imagine what you can do with this quality, think of Chaka Kahn's high screams at the end of *I Feel For You* or *Through the Fire*; think of West End sounds like the recorded version of *On My Own* from *Les Miserables*; think of the bright, 'baby' Twang sounds of most Disney heroines – Belle's opening number from *Beauty and the Beast* or *Reflections* from *Mulan*; think of Hank Williams singing *I'm So Lonesome I Could Cry*; or Patti LaBelle twanging out the high notes in *Lady Marmalade*.

Belt quality

I think it's always good to look at Belt quality after first having looked at Twang, since having grown accustomed to the feel of Twang production, you will find it easier to determine just what Belt is. And for many, it is a confusing quality. Often we describe a Twang sound as a Belt, because the two can be very similar in terms of power (in fact, Belt is a combination of Twang and Speech qualities). Also, many singers have a very 'twangy' sound in their Belt quality. On one level, it doesn't really matter, if you can produce the sound you want and if that sound is sustainable for you. But I think it's important for my students to know what Belting is, and where they can use it, since I think it's a quality you must choose with some wisdom.

PRACTICE

At its simplest, Belting is much the same sensation as calling out to someone at a distance, but with pitch, sustain and (sometimes) vibrato added. When you're Belting you feel the sound much more in your chest, but you will also be aware of much muscular energy needed in the head and neck as well. When the volume is really high, or the pitch in the upper part of the register, it feels as if the whole of your upper body is involved in making the sound, so it's a very 'physical' quality.

1. Combine sound with a little movement. Imagine you see a friend across a wide boulevard – but they are looking out of a first floor window. With a vigorous wave, look up and shout 'ay! Or 'yay!' to them.

2. Hang on to the sensation, and now press your hands together in front of your chest. Keep your elbows close to the side of your body and press so that you feel muscles in your chest and back working.

3. Call out again and this time call 'Ay, Ay, Ay!'(or 'Yay', 'Yay', 'Yay!') – and hold each sound for about 5 seconds.

4. Before you go further, check to see that while you're definitely aware of feeling effort in your neck and chest, you don't feel *strain*.

5. Call 'Ay/Yay' again three times, holding onto the sound and letting the pitch rise to the highest comfortable note, but keeping
all this sound well within your middle range.

You should have noticed that:

1. While you could feel muscle helping, you didn't really need too
much air. If you were breathing too deeply, go back and try again.
Belt doesn't need a lot of air.

2. The sensation was really centred in your chest. You felt effort in
and around the larynx, but not strain. And unlike in Twang, there
was little sensation in the nose or the facial mask area.

3. The sound – especially as you kept the hands pressed hard
against each other – was powerful.

4. If you did this for long, you may have felt a bit tired.

Listen to CD example 6 and see if your sound quality was similar.

For most singers, accessing or producing Belt isn't much of a problem. Sustaining it *can* be, because although so much of what you do in this quality is
similar to what you do in Twang, the big difference is in the mass of the vocal
folds: where Twang is sometimes thin-fold, Belt is always thick-fold. This is
why in many cases, it can sound very much like just a more musical version
of calling out to a friend across the street.

Belt often becomes very difficult to sustain in the upper range, and this is
where most singers either stop, switch into their neutral thin-fold voice
(usually calling it their 'head' voice), or – if they've listened to much Rock or
Gospel music – spontaneously carry on, having switched into Twang quality.

For the listener, it can be hard to tell the difference between Belt and
Twang – that's not so important, and these qualities are often 'mixed' anyway.
What *is* important is being able to tell the difference as the singer. You should
be able to *feel* the difference. If you're producing loud, high sounds with
relative ease, and are able to sustain that for some time, the chances are you
are Twanging. If you can produce loud sounds through your lower and mid-

range but don't feel comfortable sustaining that for too long, you're probably Belting. Twang is often experienced in and around the head, whereas Belt is generally felt in the upper chest area. Belt often has a less nasal sound to it, but it can just as often have the same kind of brassy tone as Twang. Each voice brings different harmonics to the quality and this is why the listener can get so confused when hearing Belt/Twang.

One of the easiest ways to tell the difference is to go back and access Twang though one of the exercises described above. In its 'raw' state, Twang can sound very unpleasant. Belting, because it is closer in tone to thick-fold or speaking, may be loud, but doesn't usually ever sound unpleasant to the singer – it tends to sound simply like a very loud, more musical version of their speaking voice.

Think back to the pillow and the bricks, and you'll know that using Belt can be harder, generally, on your voice than thin-fold qualities. Because of its great volume, it can be much harder on your voice than neutral thick-fold quality. It is one of the more extreme sounds you can use as a singer – but that doesn't mean you shouldn't use it. Popular music is full of Belters – you simply have to know how to blend this quality with others in order not to overuse it.

A lot of voice teachers panic about Belting, and consequently panic their students about it as well. I believe that most singers instinctively know when they are producing a sound in a healthy way; when they aren't, their voices usually let them know. If you are attempting loud sounds and find that your voice goes hoarse soon afterwards, it's time to seek some guidance. But don't let that put you off experimenting – it's fine to try things out. In fact, it's part of the process of maturing as a singer. You simply have to be smart about it and make sure that you're not constricting as you produce the tone. If you are ever in doubt, or feel that your voice 'goes' quickly, see a voice tutor who can listen and advise – preferably one who is sympathetic to the kinds of music and vocal qualities you're interested in learning.

The 'dangerous' qualities

There are a few qualities common to popular singing that I am listing as 'dangerous', simply because to many voices they are. As noted earlier, much of what we respond to in popular music has little to do with 'proper' vocal production or pleasing sound. In the BBC listener's survey mentioned earlier, 'Voices of the Century', there were few surprises in terms of the popularity of the vocalists cited (with Sinatra, Presley, Nat 'King' Cole and Ella

Fitzgerald topping the list). But it is interesting to note how many singers within the list employ qualities that I would list here as dangerous. Freddie Mercury (10), Louis Armstrong (16), Stevie Wonder (26), Robert Plant (36), Bono (38), Otis Redding (48), Tina Turner (52), Sting (59), Rod Stewart (62), Meat Loaf (64), Little Richard (75), Howlin' Wolf (80), Bruce Springsteen (85), James Brown (86), and Tom Waits (92) all employ vocal techniques – with varying rates of frequency – that involve some kind of constriction. Because so little is known about why constriction affects individual voices so differently, it is rare that the average voice teacher would want to try it with pupils. While the resilience of each voice varies, prolonged constricted vocal sounds can result in lasting damage – and if used over a number of years, they almost certainly will. As we know, that damage is often what attracts us to particular kinds of vocal sounds, so this area is fraught with peril – but no book on popular singing style can avoid recognising it.

In terms of voice qualities – which is to say in terms of a sustained, 'sung' sound – there are probably three distinct dangerous qualities, most of which are used as a small percentage of the singer's overall vocal expression. The first is what I call a Rumble – although some might call it a growl. Rumble sounds seem somewhat old-fashioned now, but were once a mainstay of Blues singing. The Rumble is more or less the sound of Louis Armstrong's vocal quality. Apart from trying to imitate Louis Armstrong, or listening to the old recordings of Bessie Smith and trying to imitate her growling sounds, the only key to accessing the sound that I've found is to think of the physical sensation of gargling – but keeping the 'gargle' low in your throat (if you don't, you may just end up sounding like you're underwater!) If you set up the sensation of gargling low in the throat and then try to sing 'through' that feeling, you'll probably be able to produce a Rumble sound. For most vocalists, this is a sound that can only be used sparingly. It will quickly dry out your throat and, if sustained for long, make your voice feel tired and rather 'croaky' afterwards – although this is usually a short-term effect. Rumble is more often used as an onset (see below) because it takes such a toll on the voice, but whether used in sustaining an entire line of a song or only in the onset, it raises the perceived effort-level of the singer and gives a kind of high-energy immediacy to a performance.

The second 'dangerous' quality is a 'creak', sometimes called 'scratch'. Creak is a dry sort of quality; it can be either pitched or not pitched. In order to access it, you can try making a noise, deep in the throat, which sounds like a creaking door. It will sound raspy, and not necessarily 'pitched' in any sense.

Some people can access this sound by talking until they reach the very end of their breath capacity and the raspy noise at the end of that very long phrase is usually a Creak. Is doesn't take much energy to sustain the Creak sound, which is why it usually appears at the final stage of the breath. Like the Rumble, this sound is most common as an onset or decay (see below), but some artists – Kenny Rogers and Lyle Lovett are probably the clearest examples of this sound – use it mid-phrase and can sustain the sound for surprisingly long periods of time. Creak is also called 'vocal fry' when it occurs right at the bottom of your range, and given its sound, this is understandable. But unlike 'vocal fry', creak can be used throughout much of the range. As noted, it's a dry sort of sound and can dry you out if you try to sustain it for long – although as noted above, some voices can sustain it just fine and still switch into a strong, clear tone at will. It can sometimes involve singing on after the breath supply is nearly exhausted, or a quick lowering of effort/breath in order to create the sound mid-phrase. The effect in performance is one of vulnerability and intimacy.

The last 'dangerous' quality is even more difficult to describe in terms of access, and that is a Constricted quality – which is, of course, singing while the false folds are a bit constricted. Many Rock and Blues singers do this quite consciously to raise the effort-level of their performance and to take the voice to extremes when expressing emotion. You will recall that we tried this earlier in the practice exercise on page 26. You may have managed it, or you may have found that not much sound came out at all. There are clearly varying degrees of application of Constriction amongst Pop singers. In some voices it can sound, temporarily, like an imitation of Rod Stewart or Janis Joplin. Some singers can temporarily constrict a tone to give a gurgling or raspy sound to the sustain and then follow on with a clear, full and unconstricted tone without doing any apparent damage to the voice. Many singers use this quality in small bursts to drive up the perceived effort-level of their singing, to match either the volume/energy of the band or the emotional intensity of a given song. The overall effect is one of raw, unmediated emotion.

Only experienced singers should experiment much with these kinds of sounds, since you can only know what your voice will or won't sustain when you're extremely familiar with the way in which it responds to fatigue or any kind of new vocal production techniques. For this reason, it's probably best that you start simply by listening to some of the examples listed in the Resources section. If you decide to try out any of these 'dangerous' qualities you should do so only with caution – and only when you're sure you can assess for yourself whether a little experimentation is sustainable. While most singing teachers will shudder at this suggestion, the pop industry is now, and has since its earliest days, been filled with vocalists who can and do sustain some constriction in their style, and many have been able to do so for the whole of their careers. There are also a great many popular singers who are not interested in the 'rules', and who want to discover for themselves what kinds of sounds they can make. We know, of course, that most singing teachers wouldn't tolerate Little Richard. Then again, we can be pretty sure that Little Richard wouldn't tolerate most singing teachers ...

Summary

Having spent a little time considering these sounds, you might agree with me that when it comes to popular music, most voices remain largely in the common neutral thin- or thick-fold range, and that many memorable voices use the other qualities – Aspirate, Belt, Twang, Elongated, Rumbled, Constricted, etc. – for greater emotional impact as well as vocal shaping and shading. As such, they often aren't pleasant qualities – especially in their raw state, which is how you have been hearing and working with them while going through this chapter. For vocalists they are anything but 'neutral'; they are the wilder, more interesting parts of the vocal palette, which can create the vocal equivalent of an expressionist painting as opposed to a gentle watercolour landscape.

The difficulty in looking at these varying qualities in isolation is that singers rarely ever use them this way. Most voices create their own spontaneous 'mix' of sounds, which means it can be a challenge sometimes to identify all the qualities a singer like Tori Amos is using. There are also a number of different descriptions used for these qualities by different teachers. What I've presented here is a guide to the kinds of sounds you're most likely to encounter in listening to popular forms like Pop, Blues, Jazz, etc.

Experimenting with sound and varying your voice qualities in unexpected ways can help you find a much greater range of vocal expression. Most of the singers I work with want to find ways to be distinct; to create a style that is both an extension of their interpretative ability and of their own personal 'take' on the world. Singing a song pleasantly, or 'correctly', is not necessarily the aim of studying popular stylistics, which is why popular style can be so difficult for traditional singing teachers to take on.

PRACTICE

The totality of the vocal qualities we've explored are best understood through practice – and that practice is best linked with the
imagination. We're going to try a practice in two parts.

1. We're going to take the first lines of *Swing Low, Sweet Chariot*:

   Swing Low, Sweet Chariot, comin' for to carry me home
   Swing Low, Sweet Chariot, comin' for to carry me home
   I looked over Jordan and what did I see comin' for to carry me
      home?
   A band of angels comin' after me, comin' for to carry me home

2. In a comfortable key (C usually works for both men and women
   – you'll find it on the CD as track 23), sing the verse through once
   in either one or a combination of the neutral thin- or thick-fold
   voice qualities. Don't think about performing it, just sing it
   through in the most comfortable neutral quality. Try this twice.

3. Now, before you sing through again, take a look at the lyrics and
   choose four phrases which you will sing with four different voice
   qualities. Because you'll be busy thinking about producing the
   voice qualities, it's best to choose your phrases and qualities
   before trying to sing. Mark the lyrics like this:

   ---

   aspirate
   Swing Low, Sweet Chariot, (comin' for to carry me home)

   elongated
   (Swing Low, Sweet Chariot,) comin' for to carry me home

   belt
   I looked over Jordan (and what did I see) comin' for to

   carry me home?

   Twang
   (A band of angels) comin' after me, comin' for to carry

   me home

   ---

4. Don't think too much about what quality goes where – this is a totally random exercise at the moment. The exercise will probably sound a bit mechanical, precisely because it *is* so random. Don't worry about that right now, just mark at least four phrases with different voice qualities. Here is a blank lyric for you to mark in your own way:

Swing Low, Sweet Chariot, comin' for to carry me home

Swing Low, Sweet Chariot, comin' for to carry me home

I looked over Jordan and what did I see comin' for to

  carry me home?

A band of angels comin' after me, comin' for to carry

  me home

Sing the piece through now, alternating between your 'neutral' voice and the other qualities you've chosen. Do it this way a few times until you're comfortable switching vocal qualities pretty quickly. *Don't try to make the switches smooth – be as abrupt as you can.*

5. After you've grown comfortable with trying this a few times, decide which parts of the verse or chorus carry the greatest emotional connection to your heart – or which you want us to have the greatest emotional response to – and go through again. Reassign the vocal qualities to different phrases if you like, and try to use whatever feels to you like the more dramatic ones (also using your heart and head!) to bring greater life/colour to those parts. Make sure the quality switches are still *very abrupt* – don't worry about being 'correct' or careful.

You should notice that:

1. The more you get used to switching vocal qualities, the more interesting your performance sounds.

2. If you are already used to switching qualities quite a lot, you may have found this the easiest exercise in the book so far!

3. When connected to your sense of performance or emotional truth, the qualities take on a much deeper and satisfying sound than when we worked through them earlier.

4. Your performance didn't sound 'schooled' or trained – and it may have sounded a bit wild.

5. If you used the predominantly high effort-level qualities (Twang, Belt, Rumble, Constricted or thick-fold) you may have felt you were singing a Rock or Blues version of your song.

6. If you used the predominantly low effort-level qualities (Aspirate, neutral thin-fold, Elongated, Creak) you may have felt you were singing a Jazz or Pop version of your song.

7. If you switched wildly from high to low effort-level sounds you may have felt that you were singing an R&B or Gospel version of your song.

8. However you worked it, your 'quick switch' version of the song should have proved more interesting to create (and to listen to!) than your initial neutral-quality version.

THE COMPLEMENTARY ELEMENTS OF STYLE

Sound, shape, effort and the elements of style

Sound and shape

Although this part of the book is all about sound, it might help to think about it as focusing on how we *shape* sound. Sometimes, when I'm trying to describe this in workshops, I use the metaphor of shapes and it seems to make sense to a lot of my students. They understand (once we've done a fair amount of listening to and talking about what makes up vocal style) what it means when we refer to a 'short thin' shape to a phrase, or a 'baggy' shape to a phrase. While we always start our work by exploring the sounds we can make in various vocal qualities, we then go on to look at how we shape that sound – and for me, the more interesting the shape, often, the more interesting the sound. The voice qualities we've been looking at are, of course, a primary part of the singer's sound; for most students who are working with a teacher to train their voices, this is where a great majority of the work takes place. The difficulty for those vocalists or singing teachers who want to be able to explore popular style is that, while voice qualities can be more or less suited to a given popular style, they are certainly not the whole picture: there are many 'complementary elements' that frame and modify those voice qualities.

These complementary elements are what give shape, colour and distinction to a singing performance, and they will be the focus of this section.

In workshops, we often begin by considering the kinds of things we've been told about vocal 'shape' at classes we've attended – either in choral or solo singing. Most of us think immediately of descriptions like 'line' or 'arc' of the melody, and generally think that the way to create a 'good' line or arc in a melody is to make a sort of gentle 'hill' out of our sound. In other words, we allow the sound and the effort to rise gradually up towards the crest of this little 'hill' and then allow it to descend gently as we ease off the phrase. I usually find that when I ask students to try to sing a line or two from a song as beautifully as they can (and I let them determine what beautiful means to them in this context), they tend to try and make these little hills of vocal shape. Of course we can make these little hill shapes in any vocal quality, but most students decide that 'beautiful' means either the neutral or the Elongated vocal qualities that we practised in the last chapter. Popular singing requires not only that you have the courage to move away from these 'beautiful' voice qualities occasionally, but also that you abandon any ideas you may have about creating the 'right' shape in a line or phrase. In fact, as we go through our exercises here, you'll discover many different ways to create interesting shapes in your sound – and with enough practice you'll find that often, your most engaging and unique vocal work will come when you've learned to create anything *but* 'gentle hills' of sound.

Effort-level

This is often referred to by singing teachers who want their students to be aware of how much (or how little) they're working while singing. However, effort-level is not commonly taught as an element of style – and it should be, because it is a major factor in the way in which we are affected when listening to a singer's performance. In some styles we *want* to be aware that the singer is working hard; indeed, that perceivable 'hard work' is frequently what convinces us that a singer is sincere. Effort-levels influence our judgement about what kind of singer we're listening to, and usually the singer is working through a number of the complementary elements described below in order to create the impression of that effort-level. Analysing the effort-level we hear is an important first step in considering a singer's style.

But we have to analyse effort-level in two ways: the *perceived* effort-level and the *true* effort-level. The perceived effort-level isn't too difficult to ascertain, although whenever I'm doing this exercise with students (we work on a scale of 1 to 10, with 10 being the highest), we'll invariably have some bickering over where we place artists. I play some songs to illustrate the lower end of perceived effort-level – for the '2 or '3' we listen to some of the old 'smoothies' like Julie London or Bing Crosby, who sometimes sound as if they could be relaxing in a beach chair while singing rather than being in the studio or on stage. For the '9' or '10' we might listen to Tina Turner or James Hetfield (Metallica) – artists whose style is often one of sheer effort and energy.

Figuring out the true effort-level can be much more difficult. A singer like Karen Carpenter will usually fool people. Her style was one of clean, effortless beauty of tone. You might put her down in the 2/3 category when compared to someone like Bruce Springsteen or Joe Cocker. But once you try for yourself those perfectly shaped long phrases, coupled with a keen attention to diction, a sound dominated by a deep, rich thick-fold quality and often capped with that beautiful vibrato decay, you quickly find that the true effort-level can be significantly higher indeed. This is an important lesson for any singer thinking about the choices they make in creating a given style or working in a particular genre. In Rock, Gospel, and Rhythm & Blues, so much of what distinguishes these genres is that the singers use great effort and energy to perform. But vocal longevity and health can often depend on being able to learn how you can create the effect of a high *perceived* level of effort without always having to produce a high *true* effort-level. Much of our work with on the complementary elements of style below will make this clearer.

The complementary elements of style

We're going to look at and practise a number of elements:

- Onsets
- Decay or release
- Sustain and vibrato
- Phrase weight and placement
- Note attack
- Breath
- Diction
- Improvisation

As we look at these, try to keep in mind that *the purpose of all of these elements is to help you communicate your thoughts/feelings effectively*. I always worry about presenting these elements without making that point – perhaps repeatedly – because I don't believe that a singer should separate what they learn technically from what they do imaginatively. Remember that these elements are part of creating a more imaginative vocal expression. Having said that, I would suggest that as you read through, you start giving each of these a try. Some may come easily; some may not. Some may seem incomprehensible at first, so always listen to the CD demonstration (as marked against each element) and then try the lyric line written.

For all the CD demonstrations, I'll be using the three traditional spirituals (*Swing Low, Sweet Chariot; Oh Freedom* and *His Eye is on the Sparrow*) I used earlier to demonstrate voice qualities. These songs have great flexibility and can sound wonderful in nearly any vocal style, so they are particularly handy for this purpose; they are also songs that many people know and sing along with easily. Listen and *imitate!* But remember – in each of these examples, the use of each element is exaggerated and repeated to help you identify the sound. This means the examples on the CD won't add up to very tasteful performances. Don't worry about that for now – we'll look later at how artists put combinations of these elements together to create a more artistic expression.

Onset

Onset is the way in which you begin the sound. Most singing teachers work with three standard onsets, often linking those onsets with given voice qualities. In my experience, that can sometimes help students to actually access the sound of those qualities. These three onsets are Glottal, Aspirate, and Simultaneous, and they are onsets that anyone can master.

ASPIRATE ONSET

This is the onset you will have used in creating Aspirate quality. In this onset, the air actually precedes the breath, and it gives a singer's performance a softer, more tentative quality. It can be sexy or vulnerable and it always creates a genuine sense of intimacy between singer and listener.

> Listen to CD Example 7
> *If you get to heaven before I do*

SIMULTANEOUS ONSET

In this onset, the tone and the breath seem to occur simultaneously. This quality has a kind of 'neutral' sound, since it doesn't require as much effort as the Glottal onset, nor is it as distinctive an onset as the Aspirate. For this reason the Simultaneous onset has no particular emotional effect on the listener in itself – it must be coupled with other elements.

Listen to CD Example 8
Oh freedom, oh freedom, oh freedom over me

GLOTTAL ONSET

This is the most 'abrupt' onset, and we've worked with it already in creating our thick-fold sound. The easiest way to feel this onset is by saying 'uh-oh'. Try that out before listening to the CD example. You'll be able to feel that the sound at the beginning of the tone is a little edgy and well-defined. It almost feels as if the tone comes before the breath in this onset, and it will feel like an onset that requires a little more effort than the first two. Because the sound gives vowels a definite edge as you come into it, this onset, when combined with 'poppingly' hard consonants, is most useful for dynamic styles – particularly styles where you want to create a high perceived level of effort. It can sound emphatic and definite, and give the listener a sense that the artist is certain about what they're saying (singing).

Listen to CD Example 9
Oh freedom, oh freedom, oh freedom over me

Along with these onsets, I think there are four other identifiable onsets used regularly in popular music. Not everyone can master these, although some can master all. Because they can give you some interesting vocal variety, it's worth trying to get a feel for them.

'FLIP' ONSET

This onset is related to the Aspirate, since it seems that most often, when used at the very beginning of a phrase, you will be aware of the air before you are aware of the tone. You may make associations between this onset and Country music, and you may be familiar with the sound of it from hearing someone yodel. According to some singing teachers, the yodel or 'flip' sound is created when the plane of the vocal folds jumps rapidly between a thin or thick fold and an aspirate position – quickly changing qualities from thin/thick to aspirate, or the other way around. Strictly speaking, this isn't always an onset phenomenon: you can't flip into a consonant, you can only flip into the first vowel. So on a word like 'swing', you would have to voice the 'sw' consonants and flip quickly into the 'i' vowel. But it would still strike us as part of the onset in this example because it happens so quickly near the front of the phrase. Nor is it only used in onset – many popular singers use this 'flip' sound mid-phrase – Jennifer Warnes, Sarah McLachlan and Alannis Morisette come to mind immediately – and others use it frequently to move from note to note or to 'switch gears' very quickly into another voice quality. While many vocalists can't find the way to use this sound mid-phrase (any more than they can yodel – which is essentially what is required), the majority of vocalists I've worked with can learn to imitate the sound for use in onset.

The emotional quality of the sound is variable. It can sometimes be a vulnerable one if used gently and with low-effort voice qualities. But hard Rock singers use this onset to gain power and give a hard edge to the opening of a phrase. There are degrees of 'width' to the sound that can vary its effect: a slower, 'wide' Flip is almost immediately associated with Country, and has a naïve, 'untrained' sound, whereas a quick, 'narrow' Flip is more often associated with Pop music and can lend a kind of sophistication or nuance to a song. Remember when you listen to the example that you have to flip on a vowel – which means that you come into the consonant sound first and then flip quickly into the vowel sound.

Listen to CD Example 10
Why should I feel discouraged?
Why should the shadows come?

Most people can master the Flip in time, but it often takes a variety of vocal 'cues' to try and familiarise a voice with this sound. If all else fails, try a Tarzan yell! This usually helps people find the sound.

'CREAK' ONSET

As in its 'sustained' application mentioned in the chapter on voice qualities, this is another onset best understood through listening. Once you're specific-ally listening out for it, you'll be surprised by how often it is used and in how many different styles and genres. As mentioned earlier, the sensation of creating the 'creak' onset is very like the feeling you have when you speak on until you come to the end of your breath capacity and your tone breaks up into a kind of 'creaking' sound. Alternatively you may try to imitate the sound of a creaking door on an 'ah'. When you use this onset, it feels as though you're dwelling in that low, throaty, creaking area of your voice very briefly just before you come into your tone. Some vocalists can extend this Creak sound, and some seem to hit it only briefly on onset, but it is a very common sound that seems to soften the onset. It can have the emotional effect of suggesting great pain or vulnerability if coupled with low-effort-level voice qualities. Used with thick-fold or speech qualities, Creak can give a more spoken or conversational feel to a song. It always creates some intimacy between singer and listener.

There is also an 'unvoiced' Creak onset. This is where the singer actually goes through the set-up creating the Creak, but then doesn't actually voice it (or else voices it so briefly it can barely be heard). This creates a kind of breathy, moaning sound as you come into the lyric, and like a voiced Creak it creates a vulnerable, almost helpless sound (listen to the very first 'Oh freedom' on the CD example). Creak can give an almost 'unsung' sound to a lyric if combined with little or brief sustain. It is also useful for singers who want a slightly 'grittier' sound in their interpretation – it isn't a 'clean' onset.

Listen to CD Example 11
Oh freedom, oh freedom, oh freedom over me

RUMBLE ONSET

This is the onset version of the 'dangerous' quality we described as sounding like Louis Armstrong, or feeling as if you're gargling and singing at the same time. It is a very old stylistic technique (in its sustained form it can be traced right back to the very earliest Blues recordings of the 20th century), probably because for singers working without mics it was a way of driving up the power and volume as they came into a phrase. You can hear it in a slightly gentler form in the work of Stevie Wonder and Whitney Houston, where I think it's used to great effect. Most singers can't (mercifully) hold onto this sound for very long – it feels hard on the throat and sometimes makes singers cough if they carry it on too long. And it can have the same effect on the ear as it has on the throat: hard. It sounds very consciously unnatural and can be very effective in making the singer seem to be trying to convince themselves or their audience of something (think of Stevie Wonder singing 'I'm a big boy now' in *The Land of La La*), but it can also sound very playful. Many Blues and R&B singers have used this sound to heighten a sexually suggestive lyric. It appeals emotionally through humour and sensuality and it convinces the listener of a singer's inner strength and resilience.

Listen to CD Example 12
  If you get to heaven before I do
  Comin' for to carry me home

CONSTRICTED ONSET

This one is the riskiest onset, but it can be very effective in raising the perceived level of effort. It is produced by constricting the false folds quickly (think *grunt*), and then letting the pressure of air build up behind the closed folds. You 'sing through' the grunt and then quickly release the folds and the air into the (unconstricted) sound. This takes much practice, because with the exceptions noted above, you might not want to carry the constriction into your sound. It's a very popular Gospel, Blues and Rock onset as it creates the sense of power and extreme emotion. The emotional effect of this onset is to convey extreme conviction to the listener. The singer is leaving us in no doubt about how high are the emotional stakes and the level of commitment for them, and it suggests that the situation is almost too important/immediate/demanding to 'sing' about.

Listen to CD Example 13
  When Jesus is my portion
  A constant friend is he

Decay or tone release

There are many kinds of release or decay, but all have to do with the way in which the singer finishes the sound. Decay suggests a finish which fades, and release is abrupt.

VIBRATO FADE

This is a common decay used by a great majority of singers, regardless of style. Because, as noted earlier, vibrato speeds and width can vary enormously, the sounds of vibrato fade decays can also vary. It's generally a sweet way to finish your sound; it has an artful, 'sung' quality about it – although combined with other kinds of release it can have more punch. On the whole, unless the final note is held for an unnaturally long time at a high effort-level, this release usually has the same kind of 'neutral' emotional impact as the Simultaneous onset.

Listen to CD Example 14
I looked over Jordan and what did I see
Comin' for to carry me home?

ASPIRATE DECAY

Depending on how strongly the singer wants to produce the decay, this may include a full stiffening of the vocal folds (which means there is no vibrato to it), or it may just be a very 'airy' sounding thin-fold tone, which can include vibrato. Most people can master this finish but it takes some practice to use it artfully. The emotional effect can be varied – it can lend a kind of gentle or contemplative mood to a performance, and it often makes the singer sound as if they are turning the sound (and perhaps the thought) in on themselves.

Listen to CD Example 15
Why should I feel discouraged?
Why should the shadows come?

FALLING OFF THE NOTE

This release works just as it sounds: the vocalist bends the note downwards, as if 'falling off' the phrase. There may or may not be vibrato. Some singers use the 'fall' with vibrato to ease down to the next note (think of Judy Garland), so that it has a very definite place to 'fall' to, which means that it's not really a tone release in this case. Others just fall nowhere in particular. There's almost always a fade to it, but sometimes subtle. In harder Rock sounds (Bruce Springsteen or Chrissie Hynde, for example) the fall neither fades nor has vibrato. It is a deliberately 'artless' sound in singing, and its effect is always strong. It might suggest that the singer's feeling is too strong to be 'sung' about, or that the singer is more concerned with the overall musical feel of the piece than with the lead vocal. Emotionally it appeals to our sense of defiance.

Listen to CD Example 16
I sing because I'm happy, I sing because I'm free
His eye is on the sparrow and I know he watches me

'PUSHED' RELEASE

Sort of the opposite of falling off the note. It's rarer than falling off and is quite distinctive in sound. This is when the singer actually pushes the note upwards slightly, just before releasing. You can hear this commonly in singers like Kate Bush, Dinah Washington or Hank Williams, and the sound can sometimes have an almost 'flip' quality to it. It creates a high-energy sound and takes true effort to produce. This release can be both gentle (which is how you'll hear it in the CD example) or extreme – see the Resources section for suggestions on where to hear the more radical versions of this release! But whether gentle or extreme, it is always a playful and sassy sound and is such an unexpected way to finish a sung phrase that it may make an audience laugh – but that is usually because it's such a joyful sound. It's a release that has usually only been used by vocalists who are brave and secure in both their power and in the uniqueness of their style.

Listen to CD Example 17
Oh freedom, oh freedom, oh freedom over me

'COMPRESSED' RELEASE
Can simply sound as if the singer has stopped the note with no attempt to soften or ease the finish. This decay is also often combined with a fast improv fill, or a short, quickened vibrato, but it still finishes fairly abruptly – in other words, it doesn't fade. Again, this decay seems to want to defy any 'sweetness' or comfort in the sung sound. It can make a singer sound angry or defiant, or (in the case of Peggy Lee's *Fever*) can sound sophisticated and cool. Its emotional effect is varied but usually makes the singer sound strong and in control of their emotion and their sound.

Listen to CD Example 18
I sing because I'm happy, I sing because I'm free
His eye is on the sparrow and I know he watches me

GOSPEL RELEASE
This decay has a burst of air on the finish. The burst can be subtle (Michael Jackson, Sarah Vaughan) or quite strong (Jennifer Holliday, Stevie Wonder). In the case of singers with a very strong Gospel influence, like Holliday, you may even hear an added syllable on an 'ah' or 'hey' sound. This is often the sound of extreme ecstasy or pain – as if the song is not enough fully to convey the singer's feeling, which must overflow into an extra syllable or sound. Like the pushed release it quickly raises both the true and the perceived effort-levels and it takes great energy to produce. Not surprisingly, its emotional effect is

inspiring – we feel absolutely inspired, either by the singer's conviction or by their passion. It creates a sense of excitement and energy.

Listen to CD Example 19
If you get to heaven before I do
Comin' for to carry me home

CREAK DECAY

This sounds exactly like the Creak onset. Many people cannot access this sound easily, and many have difficulty using it as a 'stand alone' release of sound. More often it's used to fade the sustain of one note as the singer 'glides' into the next note. It is very effective when used, because it can have a defiant, artless quality about it that suggests a kind of pain which can't be alleviated through singing – as if the sound must melt back into a kind of never-ending agony or deep thought. It's a highly vulnerable sound that creates immediate intimacy between singer and audience.

Listen to CD Example 20
Oh freedom, oh freedom, oh freedom over me

Sustain and vibrato

In popular music, the vocalist has many options when it comes to sustain, and this is especially true in R&B, Rock and Gospel styles. For many, sustain is where we feel (either as singers or as listeners) that the biggest expression of the emotion occurs, and this is why singers who use a minimum sustain time (later Dionne Warwick, for example) often strike the listener as having more emotional distance from their material than those who exploit sustain (Shirley Bassey or Liza Minelli, perhaps). In Classical music, the singer's sustain is by and large dictated by the composer; where there are long, held notes, there is little choice for the singer in how that is done. Classical style generally requires that the singer builds to the fullest, richest sound and then eases out of that sound with a vibrato fade, creating an arc within the line.

Because much popular music isn't produced in the same way – and I'm talking here about the origin of the singer's melody line – popular singers have much control over how long they hold a note and how they choose to do it. In highly improvised styles, the singer rarely builds sustain in an even manner, and may even do a 'multiple build' of sustain within a single phrase. Lengthy sustains using thick-fold, Belt or Twang qualities or sung in a high part of the register will, of course, raise the perceived effort-level. Long sustains at low- to mid-range in less demanding voice qualities can strike the listener as relatively low effort.

Because the slow-build-to-vibrato-decay is so common, having the courage to really play with sustain is a difficult thing for many singers. No one starts out sounding like Al Jarreau or Luther Vandross – but with time, most people can add much more interest to their sound by simply experimenting with all the possibilities in their sustained notes.

The speed, width, and use of vibrato can sometimes indicate style. For example, a very fast vibrato can be acceptable in many Jazz and Rock styles, whereas a very slow or wide vibrato is almost never heard in Rock styles. The wide but evenly paced vibrato is usually most artfully employed by the big show-tune voices (Judy Garland, Barbra Streisand).

As discussed earlier, there are no 'quick fixes' for singers who want to create vibrato if it isn't present in the voice. But it's important to remember that even singers who swear that they can produce no vibrato may discover some in time if they carry on singing and begin to relax and gain confidence. Suppressing or adding vibrato to the sound has a strong effect on the listener – and learning this control can be helpful in creating the sound you want. It's hard muscle work to suppress vibrato, especially on high notes, but that suppression can bring a kind of purity of emotion to a sound and give a terrific 'relief' to the listener (and the singer!) once the vibrato is slowly added in for a fade.

Phrase weight and placement

For many artists these choices can change from song to song, or even within a song. 'Phrase weight' is basically where you hear most of the emphasis in a phrase – and here is where it really helps to think of the 'shape' of a phrase. A good example might be the first two lines of Aretha Franklin's *Respect*: '*What you want / baby* I got it'. Because she makes such a powerful sound, I think of the phrase as sort of pear-shaped, with the heavy end coming first. Think how differently you might hear the song if she'd shifted the weight of the phrase towards the back. Of course, highly skilled improvisational artists like Aretha or Bobby McFerrin can sometimes throw the weight of a phrase all over the place – rising and falling in equal measures at times – this can give it a kind of 'baggy' shape. Some artists build a phrase towards the middle with very clean onsets and vibrato fades, and this can give a kind of oval shape to the phrase. Creak or Aspirate onsets, or decay coupled with a build midway, never feel 'rounded' in the same way; both ends of the phrase feel too thin or wispy for that.

Phrase placement is about where the vocalist actually starts the phrase against the actual ground beat of the song. Some vocalists are very even about this and sing right on the beat most of the time. Others are 'back phrasers', letting the track go on a bit before coming in. This generally compresses a phrase, but can be very effective in shaping both phrase and performance. There are times at which a vocalist will push the phrase forwards, although this is not quite as common as back phrasing: Bette Midler does this with regularity, and it gives a kind of breathless urgency to her performances. Many artists use a combination of forward/backward phrase placement to achieve a kind of ease or looseness about their interpretation.

Listen to CD Example 21 – and note that the phrases are deliberately being started behind the beat.

Now listen to CD Example 22 – and note that the phrases are deliberately being started ahead of the beat.

Now that you've heard the examples of back/forward phrase placement, play CD Example 23. Play it through once, and practise back phrasing everywhere you can. It may feel like too much – never mind, this is just for practice! Now play through again and push phrases forwards wherever you can. You may get a little lost on this one, but don't worry, just let the accompaniment hold it all together for you – you'll find your way if you go through this exercise a few times.

Note attack, breath and diction

Note attack is different from onset, in that it is not about the way in which the singer comes into sound, but about the way in which the singer actually comes into the pitch. In other words, some singers come straight onto the pitch with no variation in attack. For most Classical, Choral and Musical Theatre styles, this accuracy of note attack is important: it's clean, and it sounds 'legit'. For most popular music, though, vocalists often employ a slight upward bend in the note, which – when combined with ease and substantial sustain – is often called 'crooning' or 'sliding' and was always grounds for chastisement in my choir days. The amount of bend used varies greatly from singer to singer.

Listen to CD Example 24 – notice that the example is sung with very exaggerated 'bends' in the sound of the attack.

Breath is an area that doesn't come under much consideration in Classical music styles, since for the most part, the singer is trying not to make the breath audible. In popular music, audible breathing can be an important and relatively easy way to raise the perceived effort-level without creating any vocal stress whatsoever. We've already explored the ways in which audible breath sounds in Aspirate onsets/decays or Gospel releases can give a powerful shape to a phrase, but many singers are creative with the use of audible breath mid-phrase. Think of the ways in which Michael Jackson uses 'percussive' breath intakes on songs like *Don't Stop Til You Get Enough*: he's a master in using breath to create style and effect. You'll have a masterclass in breath and improv if you listen to Bobby McFerrin doing almost anything – but you can start with *Thinkin' About Your Body*, where he incorporates the very audible breath with the overall pattern of his performance. Remember that audible breath can 'up' the perceived effort-level without putting any strain at all on your voice – so be bold about using this technique if you can!

Diction can tell you a lot about the way in which an artist sees their material, and what they're actually trying to achieve with it. 'Storytellers' (Frank Sinatra, most Musical Theatre and Folk singers) always value the lyric and work hard to make the listener understand it all. Some people's accurate diction can still operate within a relatively relaxed, low perceived effort-level – and Sinatra is a case in point. Others, however, can so hammer a consonant that you are deeply aware of the energy it takes to get it out, or else hang on to the consonant in what can almost feel like Herculean effort. 'Atmosphere' vocalists like Rickie Lee Jones or Tom Waits go for an overall sonic ambience and don't worry too much about how many times you have to listen to get the lyric. They generally aim to paint a mood or picture with their songs and the mood can be enhanced by a kind of mumbling delivery. With a singer like Rickie Lee Jones, the perceived effort-level can sometimes seem low because of her soft consonants, but because Tom Waits has such a constricted quality to his voice, the perceived effort-level seems high whatever he does with his diction.

Improvisation

This can be one of the most intimidating areas for a singer, and particularly for those who are used to reading music as it is written. Improvisation applies not just to patterns of notes or alternative melody lines, but also to some of the other elements we're exploring – sustain, phrase weight and placement, and note attack. I've often thought that my own tendency to improvise was born out of the sheer boredom of singing the same songs six nights a week in clubs when I was younger. In order to improvise well, a singer must be very comfortable with the harmonic structure of a song and feel as if they know it inside out – and singing the same songs six nights a week will certainly do that for you! It's possible, of course, to improvise over any structure, but more complex chord patterns require a terrific ability to anticipate the sound of the change before it comes. I think that only happens when you've heard a song enough (i.e. many, many) times.

Most vocalists have some 'natural' improvisational tendencies – and for the most part these tendencies include a descending melodic pattern. Improvising with an ascending melodic pattern is far less common and is a lot trickier. Minimal, easy, or very logical sequences which are evenly weighted are often associated with the old Big Band/Jazz singers (Rosemary Clooney, June Christy) or a lighter R&B sound (Peabo Bryson, Denise Williams). Big octave swoops and glides, massively weighted or extended fills tend to belong to the R&B/Pop or Gospel singers (Aretha Franklin, Patti LaBelle, Christina Aguilera). Highly complex intervals and detailed or complex percussive fills remain mostly in the R&B or Jazz areas (Rachelle Ferrell, Ella Fitzgerald, etc). Trademark riffs, or repeated vocal improvisation patterns can often help you identify the singer (Mariah Carey, Sam Cooke).

To begin with, it's good to understand what your own natural patterns are. Feeling comfortable in what you're doing is always a good place to start, but you won't want to stay in that 'comfort zone' for long if you really want to create some excitement in your sound.

Many of the older Jazz vocalists (Ella Fitzgerald, Billie Holiday) have said that listening to instruments, rather than voices, taught them much about how to improvise freely. That's a good place to begin, especially since instrumental improv is almost always more daring in terms of rhythm and far more 'percussive' in that sense. Spend some time listening to instrumental improvisation (listen to any instrumental Jazz tracks you can lay your hands on with ease). Most students find it easier to think of improvising like an instrument if they are specific about *what* instrument they want to imitate – i.e. trumpet, guitar, sax, etc. It's especially good to imagine your voice improvising as different instruments: the kind of notes and rhythms you'll find for improvising like a trumpet are very different from what you'll find if you're improvising like a guitar. Find a backing track (the rise of karaoke has made this pretty easy – but I've also listed some Jazz instrumental ideas in the Resources section) to a couple of songs you know well, and improvise. Be patient – you'll make a lot of mistakes. Also be prepared to make some strange sounds, and try to be sure you'll not be heard – you'll only feel free to experiment if you know that no one is listening. You'll only learn by trying (and laughing!) and trying again. The most important thing to remember is to *work through your boredom threshold*. It is probably the hardest thing of all to do, but unless you keep at it – well beyond the usual practice time you might spend with a song – you simply won't identify all the possibilities in the song.

Remember that you have a number of elements to explore in improvisation. I'm reluctant to advise people to imitate another singer's improvisation – it almost never works. You'll notice that I've not included CD examples for improv; this is because the joy of improv lies in its spontaneous nature. As a listener, I am always uncomfortable hearing a singer try to do another singer's improv – the sound of imitation takes all the spontaneity out of the performance. I do, however, think it's a perfectly good idea to imitate an instrumentalist's improv – in fact I think you should feel free to try Miles Davis anytime!

PRACTICE

To explore melodic improvisation for a specific song, I usually ask my students to do the entire song without ever singing the melody. They invariably find this a difficult exercise and the first few times through they usually find a few 'home' notes that seem to work for long stretches of time. It takes time and courage to move away from these 'home' notes and really explore what else is possible. You can try this either with karaoke backing tracks (as long as you know the songs really well and have a passion for singing them), or you can simply sing along with a recorded piece – but never landing on the same note as the singer. In other words, sing all around the recorded artist – find different notes and seek out the gaps in the singing that you can fill yourself. You can also try singing anything but the melody against the CD accompaniment on track 25. You must always remember that improvisation – either with or without lyric – is about communicating – and the purpose of this exercise is to make sure you have a reason for doing it. Sing the song through a few times just as you know it, and then sing it through without ever using the melody with which you are familiar. You must be patient enough to do this until you've gone over it so many times that it seems simple. Once it feels (relatively!) easy to do, that's the point at which you'll find going back to melody is really interesting. You should find both relief and liberation in your performance, because you'll feel much more confident about where you can go both within and without the melody. And that's when you'll really find out where — or if — improvisation can help you to communicate more effectively than you could by singing the melody line as written.

However, not all improv is about changing or 'decorating' a melody – there are other things to consider in making a song your own.

PHRASE WEIGHT

See what happens when you change or add a weighting in your usual phrasing of a song. Try 'breaking up' even passages of phrasing in this way and find out what it does to the sound and how it affects your breathing.

BREATH

Use the breath in improv, and not only in percussive sounds or onsets/decays. Find out what happens when you force the sound through more than one phrase, right to the end of your capacity. You'll not only get some interesting tones, you'll almost certainly create an audible intake. Try this a couple of times until you find a comfortable way to use it in a song – it's a good way to raise the effort-level without stress.

PHRASE PLACEMENT

Be bolder about where you come into the song – let the music carry you for bit before you enter. Don't sustain so much – it will give you time to think of more interesting places to start in again. See what happens if you come in before the count of 1. You'll get lost sometimes as you're starting, but learning how to phrase in less even ways can make your delivery much more interesting.

SUSTAIN

See what happens when you consciously try to change your sustain pattern. If you tend towards the 'classical' slow-build-to-vibrato fade, find out what happens when you mix those elements up. Try building and then releasing with a compressed decay. Try multiple builds in the sound. See what happens when you start the vibrato fade and then suppress the vibrato into a 'falling' decay. There are many combinations you can try – and no doubt some of them will sound strange to you at first, but stay with it. Interesting singers rarely do things the obvious or 'even' way.

DICTION

If you're used to singing with very clean diction, see how the song sounds if you relax that as far as you're able to and concentrate much more on varied and interesting onsets and decays/releases.

The amount of work you can do in this way is unlimited – and all of it will pay off. Any singer with a relatively good ear will progress quickly with some dedicated practice. But be warned: it's not a linear process. In other words, you don't begin and end it like a lesson; it's something that you need to keep going back to in order to keep increasing your confidence. Good, imaginative improvisation is a key to many popular styles and it can make the difference between a good singer and an exciting one. This process is also a good one to go through in a student/teacher context – it allows for much more play and feedback and will give both of you a starting point when trying out things like a Pop or Jazz piece.

A summary practice

Our final practice will involve trying out as many of the various vocal qualities and complementary elements as we can. You can use this part of the book as a 'workbook', as we review all the materials from sections 2 and 3.

Begin by putting a tick next to every voice quality you were able to do (go back and review if you've forgotten any of the 'access keys'!):

- ❏ Neutral thin-fold
- ❏ Neutral thick-fold
- ❏ Aspirate
- ❏ Elongated
- ❏ Twang
- ❏ Belt
- ❏ Creak
- ❏ Rumble
- ❏ Constricted (watch this one carefully and don't do much – even if you're relatively comfortable with it!)

Now put a tick next to every onset you were able to imitate successfully:

- ❏ Glottal
- ❏ Aspirate
- ❏ Flip
- ❏ Creak
- ❏ Rumble
- ❏ Constricted (again, careful with this – even if you have it comfortably, you may not have had enough practice to do it safely for long)

Tick every decay or tone release you were able to do with relative ease:

- ❏ Aspirate
- ❏ Falling off the note
- ❏ Pushed
- ❏ Compressed
- ❏ Gospel
- ❏ Creak

You will notice that I didn't include some of the easier elements. This exercise is about really experimenting with sound, and *not* about playing safe.

PRACTICE

On the blank lyric sheet below, do the following:

1. At the beginning of the lines, mark in as many onsets as you can (at least 3).

2. At the end of the lines, mark in as many tone releases or decays as you can (at least 3).

3. Choose 4 phrases and bracket them. Now mark in at least 4 voice qualities over the bracketed phrases.

4. Put BP (Back Phrase) or FP (Forward Phrase) at the beginning of at least 2 lines – and a further line if you can.

> Swing Low, Sweet Chariot, comin' for to carry me home
>
> Swing Low, Sweet Chariot, comin' for to carry me home
>
> I looked over Jordan and what did I see comin' for to
>
> carry me home?
>
> A band of angels comin' after me, comin' for to carry
>
> me home

Your marked-up lyric sheet should look something like this:

> flip
> Swing Low, Sweet Chariot, (comin' for to carry me home) asp   aspirate
> BP (Swing Low, Sweet Chariot,) comin' for to carry me home creak   Twang
> glottal I looked over Jordan and what did I see (comin' for to   BP   Belt
>
> carry me home?) compressed
>
> creak   BP
> A band of angels comin' after me, (comin' for to carry   FP   Twang
>
> me home) gospel

Now, using CD Example 23, go through the verse, and try to do every marked quality and element on the page. This is a purely random exercise, and it's going to sound *random*. That's okay. We need to get used to making the noises before we can do anything else with them. There is only one rule here: make your voice quality changes abrupt – don't try to smooth them out or go into them elegantly. Let them be as quick and artless as you can. Go through this at least three times. Enjoy the sounds you're making – they will probably be a bit strange to you at the moment.

Once you're feeling more secure at just making the sounds in the right places, go back and look closely at the lyrics. The song is about things that all of us can relate strongly to – about freedom and redemption and going home to some place safe and secure, being with people we love. Think about what you really want to communicate when you sing the song. Do you want us to feel comforted or inspired? Should we feel confident that you'll survive? Should we *help* you survive? Try to connect the meaning of these words to your heart and your head. Speak the lyrics through once and see if you can make your meaning clear. Now play the CD accompaniment and go through the song one more time with all your voice qualities and elements intact. Keep all your voice quality switches abrupt. This time after you've gone through, you may feel you want to change where you've put some things. Take a bit of time and switch things around if you want, *but don't lose the number of qualities or elements you're doing.* Sing through again, really holding onto to the things that give the song meaning for you. If you're feeling happy with what you've tried, go on to CD Example 25 – which is the same accompaniment, but has a looser, slightly more jazzy sound. That may inspire you to connect even more closely with both what's in your head/heart and with the kinds of sounds you're making.

I do this exercise in workshops, and I'm almost always amazed at the results. While we rarely ever achieve great artistry, there is almost always something extraordinary in what we hear. That is partly because it takes real bravery to sing like this, and also because the singers in the workshop are not concerned with pleasing anyone or sounding beautiful. That means that whatever we think of their final performance, we usually find it moving and engaging. Even though the exercise begins in a completely random way, if the singer keeps holding on to what they feel in their own hearts about the song, they usually manage to get that across to us in a variety of ways — which does much to take the randomness of the exercise away. Wherever you land with this exercise, you're bound to have made some singing choices you wouldn't ordinarily have made, and you're bound to have explored outside your usual ideas of 'good' singing. That in itself is a good beginning for exploring who and what you can be when you sing!

HEARING VOICES

How to listen to and analyse a singer's performance

While learning to practise and perform the elements of style is a great way to expand your expressive ability as a vocalist, listening to the ways in which other artists put these elements together is just as important. In this section I want to lead you through the works of a number of artists in different genres, which I hope will help to make the relationship between our isolated look at the elements and the art of combining and employing them artfully a little clearer. In the interests of brevity, most of the analyses of the songs covered in the sections below are quick – they're meant to increase and deepen your knowledge of how singers have worked in various genres. Singers grow their own style best when remaining open to the widest possible range of influences, so try to keep an open mind as we go through even the kinds of music you think you don't like.

Before getting to these sections on genre, I think it important to spend a bit of time looking in detail at one recording. It will help to consolidate the ideas we've covered so far and it's a good way to establish your vocabulary in the elements of popular style while you listen.

I've chosen a song by Whitney Houston to start with – *Saving All My Love*

For You. It's pretty easy for most people to get a copy of this recording, and the song features a good range of the stylistic elements we've been looking at, all of which are pretty clear and easy to distinguish. Before all else, I want to suggest that when listening, what you're doing is gathering the signs a singer gives you in order to be able to answer the bigger question: 'What is the singer trying to communicate with this song?'

This, of course, is the question you will always have to ask yourself as a singer – what am I trying to do/say with this song? What do I want my audience to think/feel when it's finished? These questions lie at the root of a great singing performance. Sometimes a singer wants to make us cry, or to make us feel the depth of their pain; some singers want to educate us; or want our sympathy. There are times when a singer wants to make us laugh; or wants to share their philosophy about some part of life, and to convince us of its importance. There are singers who want to make us believe in something, or who want surprise us; singers who want to frighten us, shock us perhaps, or who want to laugh at us. Often singers simply want to remind us that we're not alone in our pain or in our joy, and to remind themselves that they're not alone either. And some singers simply want to use a song to sound like someone else, or to impress us with their technical skill. The greatest singers probably do all of this and more at various stages throughout their careers. But whatever it is that the singer wants to communicate, it really does need to be specific in their hearts and minds.

This becomes, in an actor's language, the 'intention' of a song. And the way in which the singer chooses to make that intention clear will have everything to do with the stylistic choices available to her or to him.

Not every singer is aware of singing with such specific intention – but most are aware of wanting to make some kind of statement with their work. As you're listening to Whitney Houston, you might try to figure out just what it is she wants to *do* with this song. Because there are many subjective elements in anyone's response to a song, it's not important whether we agree on all the conclusions I might draw in listening to this song. It's simply important that you get used to articulating your own views through a vocabulary of vocal style.

Saving All My Love For You

You'll need to locate a copy of this recording – it's easily downloadable on iTunes. As you listen to the song, follow the marked lyric sheet, which provides a helpful demonstration of all the elements we've been listening to and practising, but pulled together in the context of a great Pop/light R&B performance. It will take you a little time to get used to the shorthand for the elements I'm identifying here, but that isn't too important. If you've gone through the CD practice from the last chapter, you'll recognise most of the elements as you hear them. Because inevitably there are so many things to identify in a performance this rich, I've tried just to concentrate on the strongest sounds — you may hear many others if you listen closely.

KEY

Onset:

Aspirate **asp**

Simultaneous ><

Glottal ʊ

Flip ⊘

Rumble ⋁⋀

Releases:

Vibrato fade ⟩

Vibrato compressed ⋗

Aspirate **asp**

Falling off the note ⟩

Compressed ⊣

Pushed ⌐⌐

Gospel ⟨

Quick improvisation ⋁⋀⋀

Note attack:

Upward bend ╱

Downward bend ⟩

Vocal qualities:

Neutral thick ══

Neutral thin ──

Aspirate Ⓐ─

Belt Ⓑ─

Twang Ⓣ─

Elongated Ⓔ─

asp
A few stolen moments is all that we share ⋊
Ⓐ

⋉ You've got your family, and they need you there ⋊

Though I've tried to resist, being last on your list ⋊

But no other man's gonna do ⟹
Ⓑ

So I'm saving all my love for you ⟹
ⓉⒷ

asp
It's not very easy, living all alone ⋊

My friends try and tell me, find a man of my own ⋊

But each time I try, I just break down and cry ⋊
Ⓑ   Ⓑ

Cause I'd rather be home feeling blue ⟹
Ⓑ

So I'm saving all my love for you ⟹
Ⓑ

⋉ You used to tell me we'd run away together ⋊

Love gives you the right to be free ⟹

⋉ You said be patient, just wait a little longer ⋊
Ⓑ

But that's just an old fantasy ⟹
Ⓑ

asp
I've got to get ready, just a few minutes more
(A)

Gonna get that old feeling when you walk through that door
(B)

For tonight is the night, for feeling alright

We'll be making love the whole night through
(T)

So I'm saving all my love
(T)(B)

Yes I'm saving all my love
(T)(B)

Yes I'm saving all my love for you
(T)(B)

No other woman is gonna love you more
(B)

Cause tonight is the night
(B)

That I'm feelin' all right
(B)

We'll be makin' love the whole night through
(B)

So I'm saving all my love
(B)

Yeah I'm saving all my lovin'
(B)

Yes I'm saving all my love for you
(B)

For you, for you

Along with the notes I've provided, feel free to make your own notes as you listen – you may well hear more or different things. So what do we find when looking at the vocal choices Whitney Houston makes in this recording?

EFFORT-LEVEL

I'd say that the overall perceived effort-level is around 6/7. The verse openings have a very easy quality to them, and for the most part, you don't really feel the effort until she gets to chorus repeats. You can hear that she's working hard throughout the last repeat, so the overall effect for me is just above the middle of the scale. She uses some good, safe (i.e. not hard on the voice) elements to push the perceived effort-level up – notably by providing some strong contrast between voice qualities. Simply by switching quickly and often between contrasting voice qualities, a singer can give the impression of working hard. She's also using some heavier onsets – particularly the use of a rumbling onset on '*old* fantasy' and 'tonight *is* the night'. She also uses some big consonant sounds in the last verse of the song (you can hear how heavily she emphasises the 't' sounds in the phrases: 'cause tonight is the night / that I'm feeling all right') in a kind of staccato pattern with little sustain, since she rightly senses here that sustain would somehow ease the tension of her emotion rather than raise it for the listener.

I'd say the true effort-level is a bit higher, perhaps a 7/8 – she's doing some pretty interesting voice quality changes, and some of them are more difficult than they sound. Perhaps the greatest effort she'll be using will be on the highest note and at the end of the third repeated 'saving all my love for *you*' in the last refrain. She's using a very powerful, edgy but almost hollow-sounding thin-fold, which creates real volume but may not strike the listener as needing much effort to sustain. Actually, the tone itself isn't difficult for most singers to sustain, but coming off the Twangy thick-fold quality of 'saving all my love for' and going into this thin-fold power quality with absolute accuracy – which she holds for a very long time without vibrato – takes real muscle work. If you have any doubts about that, give it a try!

VOICE QUALITIES

She goes through quite a few, but since the overall impression you have of the song comes from the big choruses, it can feel as if the dominant quality is Belt or Twang. It isn't, though – she uses her neutral thin-fold and thick-fold qualities just as often. As mentioned earlier, it can be quite hard to distinguish exact qualities as you listen to them – it's much easier to feel them when you're doing them yourself. But I think I hear some interesting quick changes, especially in the final phrase which goes: 'Yes I'm [thick-fold] saving all my love for [Belt/Twang] you [very bright thin-fold]'. The rapid change between voice qualities raises the effort-levels.

INFLUENCES

Whitney Houston comes from a comfortable, very musically influenced background (her mother is R&B singer Cissy Houston and her cousin is Dionne Warwick), and you can hear elements of Gospel, R&B, Blues, Rock and Jazz in the voice. However, the way in which she combines the elements has a kind of lightness about it – so although this certainly feels like a Rhythm & Blues track, there's none of the urgency you find in the heavier R&B singers. Perhaps the singer she reminds me most of is Natalie Cole – another vocalist who came from a relatively comfortable, very musically influenced background, who was recording a bit earlier.

ONSET AND DECAY

In this song she doesn't do very much in her note beginnings and endings that would affect the effort-levels. In the lighter, thin-fold sections she uses an Aspirate onset sometimes; only two or three times can you hear her use a 'flip' onset ['You said be patient'], and she uses the Rumble onset twice, as noted earlier. Her decay sound is dominated by the vibrato fade, which is sometimes speeded up to give a Compressed release ('Cause tonight is the night').

SUSTAIN

For the most part she saves her big heavy sustains for the chorus. When she holds the note, she generally does so with an even amount of volume. You're aware of the effort it takes to sustain on such a big sound, but because she doesn't particularly build or improvise within the sustain, the effort-level doesn't seem intense. However, she pounds her consonant sounds quite hard in these sections, which does make the listener aware of her effort.

VIBRATO

Generally her vibrato has a light feel to it. It's relatively fast and often held off until the very last of the sound – which can create a high true effort-level, and a relatively low perceived effort-level.

IMPROVISATIONAL PATTERNS

Her improvisation is light and quick and generally used for rounding off a sound – often no more than moving up or down a tone. She uses very little in the way of melodic improvisation; this is one of the things that places the song more comfortably in the Pop genre, despite its clear R&B influence.

PHRASE WEIGHT AND PLACEMENT

Her work here is very even. She is very consistent both where she starts a phrase, and how she distributes breath/energy throughout the phrase. There's no back phrasing, nor does she ever push a phrase forwards of the beat. This evenness creates a slightly lower perceived effort-level.

NOTE ATTACK

She uses a gentle upward bend in the note attack, especially in the lighter phrases.

DICTION

Her diction is very strong in the big moments, and always clean and comprehensible.

BREATH

We hear a slight breath sound on many of her releases; not strong enough to be a 'gospel' finish, but enough to suggest effort – 'mild' Gospel?

SO WHAT IS SHE TRYING TO DO WITH THE SONG?

She wants to tell a story, so she really values the lyric and is careful with diction. She's trying to make us understand that the life of a mistress is a hard one, and perhaps trying to convince us not to judge so quickly. She doesn't overwhelm the song with a sense of her pain, but we're never allowed to forget it. She seems to want to convince us that for all the emotionally charged circumstances of the song, she doesn't want her listener to think she's abandoned her logical capacity to see the true limitation of her situation and her own culpability in it. If she had abandoned herself to self-pity here, she would, I think, have sacrificed some of our understanding.

Because she treads the middle ground, we probably respond to her both logically and emotionally. She's combining some beautiful sounds with a strong emotional charge, and neither the technical nor the imaginative side of her work is short-changed. We are also probably left wondering how to feel about this woman. For all her careful delineation of the situation, there is no doubt where her heart really is: squarely on anticipating all the joys of seeing this man, guilty or not. We draw this conclusion because it is in the moments of this anticipation in the song that Whitney Houston ups the effort-level, thereby 'upping' our sense of her involvement in the moment.

This is an early recording for Whitney Houston, and in the ensuing years, some critics have worried that she has grown more concerned with displaying her vocal virtuosity than in performing songs that seem deeply connected to her heart. But when I listen to this early track, I think she's making that connection both powerfully and skilfully.

Analysing what you hear is an important step in training your voice as well as your ear. If you can learn to hear accurately, you'll have more ideas when you produce sounds yourself. You will find that the more you listen and make your own notes on different vocal performances, the more attuned your ear becomes. That can only be helpful if your aim is to try and stretch the stylistic limits of your own performances.

Summary

In reading these last two sections, you've probably discovered that I have been suggesting two things all the way through. The first is that you have to know what you want to communicate with a song before you can think about style. The second is that although there are a great number of elements to learn and to enjoy experimenting with, perhaps what is of greatest importance to the listener is knowing that the singer *has something to communicate*. That doesn't simply mean power and passion in the voice – convincing and communicating with the listener also depends upon getting the context right. In a sense this is just common knowledge. We know that Opera requires an extreme effort-level; it is concerned with great classical themes of tragedy and the human condition. We know that traditional Musical Theatre and many of the lighter 'legitimate' styles demand diction, but also a kind of ease about their delivery. But we want to be convinced in the emotional passages, and in these parts we expect to sense real honesty in the singer's delivery. We know that Gospel singers are singing of their spiritual ecstasy, and also trying to proselytise the listener – we expect extreme connection of heart and voice here of a kind that would be utterly out of place in the usual Church of England Evensong service.

As listeners we can sometimes be put off by singers who simply sound beautiful, or singers who are singing artfully but not (as we may perceive it) soulfully or truthfully from their hearts. Increasingly, what we value in vocal music is the sense that we are being let into the singer's personal realm. We may find that in a tearful delivery (Sinead O'Connor), or we may find it in great soaring notes (Chaka Kahn); we may find it in sheer energy and bravado (Mick Jagger), or we may find it in quieter, 'creakier' sounds (Damien Rice). But wherever we find it, we will probably also find a singer who is not as concerned with 'singing' as they are with communicating.

The heart of style, then, must be in communicating as effectively as possible.

The early style artists

It's difficult to talk about good or bad voices when listening to singers like Ma Rainey, Hank Williams, Woody Guthrie, or Jimmie Rodgers. Because in a sense, these artists worked against such notions in the attempt to strip away the 'art' or artifice in their singing, and to convince the listener that their work was neither contrived nor beautified, but simply honest. One may still argue, perhaps, that these artists remained deeply concerned with the 'art' of creating a soulfully convincing sound, but they nevertheless did so with absolutely no recourse whatever to classical or traditional ideas of good vocal production.

My point here is that since the early 20th century, vocal styles (like other arts since the first stirrings of modernism) have been marked heavily by an attempt to bypass accepted ideas of 'good' or 'bad' – and, in some cases, by completely subverting the listener's expectations. This subversion was achieved against extraordinary and specific social conditions, and, if anyone has doubts about the political importance and dimension of style, a quick look through the history of Ragtime, Blues and Jazz in turn-of-the-century America will convince even the most sceptical.

This book isn't about that history, but about the effects of those stylistic changes. And I think in order to understand the choices available in contemporary singing, we need to look at those styles which found their values in a kind of gritty experiential authenticity, and those which found their values in rethinking and extending musical complexity and skills in the popular sphere. Of course, there isn't a simple division between these two approaches, but sometimes a simple model can help early understanding in a complex subject. To that end, while we're exploring some fundamental genres, we'll also be evaluating the way in which some artists were looking to communicate as simply and directly as their musical forms would allow, and some whose expressive desires were decidedly more complex.

This section will examine the various ways in which popular singers utilise the elements and qualities described in the previous sections to create an overall impression on the listener. That impression may be one that the listener 'categorises' – in other words, choices that the singer makes may relate to particular elements or qualities that are often associated by us historically with certain genres of music. For example, Belting or a strong nasal Twang, coupled with a high frequency of Flip onsets and slow bends in the note attack, are vocal qualities and elements of style that are often associated with Country music. These qualities are, of course, common to nearly every style of popular singing, but put together in this way they usually remind the listener of an identifiable Country sound.

Or it may be that the overall impression made by a vocalist on the listener isn't necessarily one that the listener 'categorises', but simply responds to in a more intuitive or emotional way. For example, most listeners, I think, would respond first emotionally to Jennifer Holliday's highly charged rendition of *And I Am Telling You I'm Not Going* before pondering whether this song belongs in the Gospel, Rhythm & Blues, or Show song category. In a sense, of course, it doesn't matter – how it all adds up to us as listeners is what counts.

For some people, a strong association with the traits of a given vocal style or genre can be the first thing that either invites or repels a sympathetic listening. Such people may feel that the overall impression of a singer as 'too Jazzy' or 'too legit' (or whatever one's preferences/dislikes may be) is so strong that they aren't persuaded to have a closer listen. Similarly, for some people, such overall impressions are what attract their interest in the first place. As noted earlier, when considering contemporary popular music it grows more and more difficult to draw such distinctions, and the wealth of easily obtainable recorded material has greatly increased the source of influence for singers.

Although such crossover and hybrid approaches in contemporary recorded music of the last 30 or 40 years has made classification in this sense more and more difficult to maintain, I believe there are still some pretty fundamental popular genres – and amongst these I would count Blues, Gospel, Jazz, Country, Rock and Vaudeville/Music Hall or Broadway styles. These all, of course, crossover themselves, and trying to follow the threads of each style back to where one might locate a 'pure' strain of style is a particularly difficult task. Perhaps of all these styles, early American Blues, Jazz and Gospel would be the most likely forms to sustain and reward such a search. In a sense, too, the very early years of Broadway and Music Hall styles (which were in essence a popularisation of Opera and Light Opera) could be said to form a fairly distinct if derivative style at some point. But while one might argue, for example, that there is a popular strain of 'legitimate' singing style that could be traced from Jeanette MacDonald or Deanna Durbin through to Julie Andrews, which remained for sometime relatively untouched by the great Jazz and Blues influences of American Popular music, it would still have to be acknowledged that there are many points at which the styles have converged. There could also be said to be strong distinctions in the early years of this century between Jazz and Blues, but such distinctions do not hold for long.

As impossible as it is to untangle the myriad threads of vocal style over the last century, it is still a compelling if puzzling pursuit. In the summer of 1999, American cable music channel, VH1 put together a list of the '100 greatest women of Rock & Roll'. If ever one needed proof that Rock & Roll is, in itself, a hybrid form, it would be in the reading of this list. In the top ten are Aretha Franklin and Tina Turner (Gospel roots), Janis Joplin (Blues/Rock), Joni Mitchell (Folk/Jazz), Billie Holiday (Blues/Jazz) and Bonnie Raitt (Country/Rock). Of the singers who remain (Chrissie Hynde, Madonna, Annie Lennox, and Carole King), only Hynde seems to fit snugly into a 'Rock & Roll' category. Madonna, Lennox and King are vocalists whose styles are much more eclectic and difficult to assign anywhere except, perhaps, 'Female Pop'.

In the following sections I'll be focusing on some specific artists and recordings. In the attempt to look at some descriptive qualities in these areas, I've largely had to avoid anything too current. In the contemporary world of fusion and crossover, it's extremely difficult to separate the 'Country' world of Shania Twain from the 'Pop' world of Avril Lavigne. This means that any effort to take an overview of such categories is bound to be a fairly historical one, and my analyses below will in most instances be of some pretty old recordings. But I believe that these early works established much about the styles under consideration and remain part of a common working vocabulary in popular music today. You will also note that I only provide detailed practice notes for the early genres – Blues, Jazz and Gospel. This is because in their early forms, they are not so 'fused' with other sounds and you can reasonably talk about and practise the things that constitute the style. For Country (which is a genre that mixed European Folk, Blues, Swing and 'Jump Blues'), and for Rock and Pop (which are fusions of all these early styles), the sections are really just to help you think about the most common elements a singer might want to listen out for and apply when exploring in these areas.

It is extremely common in a teaching situation to encounter students who would love to explore styles like Blues or Country further, but who don't have a starting point. I'm hoping that the following section, and the Resources section at the back of this book, can help to provide a lot of interesting starting points for you. One of the great bonuses of the 'information age' we're living in is that both sound and history are so much easier to come by for someone who wants to spend a little time gaining greater knowledge and confidence about vintage forms of popular music. I've come to believe that listening and imitating is still the greatest way to expand your repertoire of the elements of style. I'm often surprised when an artist mentions whom they're listening to at a given time – I'm sure I wasn't the only one who found it curious to read in a recent interview that Randy Blythe (the gloriously unique lead singer of thrash metal band Lamb of God) cited Barry White and the Pet Shop Boys as current influences. I was equally fascinated when interviewing Paul McCartney to hear of his current passion for Nat King Cole. It shouldn't be surprising though – any artist who really wants to extend their stylistic ability should have eclectic tastes.

In compiling the section below, I've tried to find familiar and unfamiliar pieces that show both the evolution of styles and also the evolution of some specific voices. I'm not listening or writing about these songs as a record reviewer – there are certainly enough of those! My concentration remains on what the style and the artist are communicating and what elements the artists are employing to achieve that communication. I also hope that in providing a relatively brief introduction to key artists in each style, those wanting both to teach and to learn will be inspired by listening to those who were indeed charting new territory and (in some cases) struggling to find their own distinctive voice and style. Great artists have always studied those who have come before them – and I hope that in discovering (or rediscovering) some of these songs, you'll find the courage to push yourself in new directions and to be brave enough to abandon whatever vocal 'safe places' you might customarily inhabit.

In a perfect world, there would be one single CD with a range of styles that I could refer to – but, alas, no such thing exists! Consequently, I've tried to concentrate on analysing recordings that should be easily available.

Fortunately, there are a lot of relatively quick and inexpensive ways to get hold of music these days, and I've tried to restrict the majority of my choices to songs that can be located with ease on iTunes. That means that with just a few exceptions you could put together an accompanying library of all the songs referred to below for about £20. I still think this the easiest way to build a little 'style library', but I know there are many who prefer CDs and will want to look for songs that way. If you refer to the Resources section at the back of the book, you'll find ideas for locating all the songs referred to below.

A NOTE ABOUT THE PRACTICE EXERCISES IN THIS SECTION

At the end of the first genre analyses I've included a bit of practical work that I use in workshops with my own students. Of course, no one 'learns' vocal style in this way. The exercises are not designed to make you a Blues singer or a Jazz singer; they are included after the listening sections to give you a practical framework for exploring your own voice and for extending the range of your possibilities. It's important to remember that we often sing in a habitual way. In doing so, we sometimes get trapped – either by our muscular memory, or by the memory of what we ourselves or others have decided sounds 'good' or 'right'. In order to expand our expressive capabilities, we need to let go of our habits sometimes and to remember the power of the unusual, the bold, the awkward and even the downright wrong/bad sounds that our voices are capable of. I think it helps to think of these exercises as the vocal equivalent of the right-handed painter I described earlier, who decided to start painting with his left hand. He didn't expect to paint a masterpiece; he was just trying to avoid painting pleasant and forgettable work. Like him, you're bound to find yourself exploring something strange – you may produce a performance that makes you laugh or you may produce something that feels liberating. Hopefully you will find some unexpected sounds that can build a more direct pathway between your heart and those of your listeners. But whatever you find, the exercises should help to disrupt some of your habitual singing patterns, and that's always a good thing if we want to keep growing as artists.

Please remember the following:

1. These are not vocal training exercises – they're not designed to be done on a daily basis. They are purely to help you explore and to encourage you to work in different, maybe bolder ways.

2. You should monitor your vocal stamina and be responsible in what you do. Don't persist in things that feel uncomfortable, and if your voice is hoarse or husky after any of these exercises, you know you'll have pushed things too much. All voices are different and some are more delicate than others. But these exercises are relatively short and if you're careful about effort-level, they should be perfectly safe to do.

3. As with any vocal exercises, remember to warm up before trying them, don't try anything if you're ill (or still recovering from illness), and make sure you have a bottle of water and that you stay well hydrated when working.

4. Working in different ways can sometimes mean that muscles get tired. Try to learn to distinguish between muscle fatigue and vocal strain. If muscles around your larynx feel tired but your voice sounds fine, you're probably extending the exercises longer than you should, or your muscles are tired from producing voice qualities or sounds that you're not used to. If in doubt about anything, reduce your effort-levels.

5. Don't panic and don't let others panic you. Permanent vocal damage takes time to achieve. Allow yourself to explore some of the sounds you're hearing, but make sure that you're only doing a little at a time with those sounds that feel really foreign to you.

Blues

'I didn't hate [Ma Rainey], she was all right, but I never cared too much for her. I seen her a lot, you know, she always sounded flat to me. When she sings, she sang flat... I never did like that kind of singing.'

Little Brother Montgomery[1]

'Oh Lord, don't say anything about Ma... Ain't nobody in the world ever yet been able to holler "Hey Bo Weevil" like her. Not like Ma. Nobody. I've heard them try to, but they can't do it.'

Victoria Spivey[2]

In a sense, considering vocal style almost always means considering what the word 'art' means — and not only in its aesthetic sense. Art is an interesting word, which grows more interesting still when you consider some of its

1 Giles Oakley, *The Devil's Music*, 2nd ed. (New York: Da Capo Press), 1997, p. 94
2 Oakley, p. 94

cousins: arty, artful, artificial. In itself, the word simply means practical skill or the application of practical skill, and we both admire and distrust it as a description. If we were to consider the idea of 'singing as art', we would probably think of the principles of Classical singing. We would probably also expect that 'art' means something mediated – something taught, learned, considered and then applied. And when we look at popular singing styles, we must admit that some styles seem to have evolved precisely in order to disrupt or subvert all that. The Blues is an 'artless' style – it is a kind of musical 'defiance'.

Blues singing is the result of a kind of historical melting pot – many influences could be traced. But the first Blues singers were male – members of the black minstrel shows who worked itinerantly throughout the south, in large tent shows, church halls, etc., always without microphone. This last point is significant since the history of vocal style is, in many ways, the history of the microphone and of sound technology generally. When we listen to contemporary vocal recording, every tiny shade of sound is available to our ears because recording technology is now so sophisticated (and some would say *too* sophisticated) that singers can move from a whisper to a roar and a good engineer can balance it all out for us so that we don't miss anything and our stereo speakers don't blow! But early microphones were either non-existent or very rough instruments, and singers had much to do to compensate for that.

With no rules at all to guide them, the early Blues singers set out to create a sound that they owned. There was an impressive variety of popular music in America at the time, and at the close of the 19th century, perhaps the three most influential were the folk songs of Stephen Foster, the ragtime sounds of Scott Joplin, and the marches of John Phillips Sousa. Recovering from the Civil War and witnessing the urban growth of industrialisation in the big cities, it is relatively easy to conclude that 'true' early Blues style – the Blues emanating from Southern poor rural black musicians – was pretty quickly assimilated by the more sophisticated vaudeville and cabaret artists of the time – and just as quickly exploited by early recording companies who found a profitable market for 'race' records.

This latter idea – that there was one market for 'race' records and another for a dominant 'white' record-buying public – had a truly profound effect on style in the history of American popular music. And because American popular music has had such international impact, the result, I would argue, is that much of what we recognise as popular music style owes its existence to a protracted struggle in the early days of recording between artists/producers/ record-company executives trying to maintain very clearly the distinction between the market for black recordings and the market for white recordings; and, on the other hand, the fairly free exchange of styles and influence that occurred amongst the artists – and the audiences – themselves. Perhaps, historically, this is not a surprise; nor would I think it too contentious to say that racial division in America has produced much culturally – both in terms of the rearguard desire to maintain cultural 'purity', and of the inevitable cross-cultural experimentation that fuels the more adventurous artists. Consequently, it is foolhardy to consider the evolution of popular singing styles in the first half of the 20th century without acknowledging the racial context in which that evolution occurred. Similarly we must acknowledge that, as the century went on, advances in sound technology changed both the live and the recorded sound of the singer. Blues singers are particularly interesting to consider in both these contexts.

The idea of the 'Blues singer' may have been a relatively new one in the early part of the 20th century, but as the quotations above show, that didn't mean that early listeners weren't applying their own aesthetic judgements to the songs. Little Brother Montgomery's assessment of Ma Rainey may have been fair (although in her recordings there are no discernible pitch problems), or it may simply have been a response to the downward inflection and general lack of sustain in her delivery that gives it a 'flat' and somewhat 'artless' style.

In its 'purer' forms, Blues singing has an extraordinarily consistent vocal heritage that can be traced with ease from, say, the earliest recordings in the 1920s of Bessie Smith right up to Etta James's 1998 collection, *Life, Love and the Blues*. Blues includes a number of distinct shadings and styles (rural, Mississippi Delta, Chicago, etc.) which, while often influencing each other, have their own identifiable kinds of vocal sounds. But perhaps what unites the form is that for the most part, traditional ideals of musicality or beauty or tunefulness are not prioritised in this work – instead, Blues singers have from the very first employed a wide variety of all the kinds of sounds that human voices make, from the piercing, to the raspy, to the raw in order to take their listeners on a highly personal journey of the heights and depths of the human soul. It's a form that actively embraces and rewards an enormous range of vocal sound.

Many early Blues songs were accompanied by guitar and banjo, and this perhaps accounts for the musically less adventurous sounds of some of the singers as opposed to those of later Blues artists who were singing with piano, bass, drums and horns. The variety and complexity of these added instruments no doubt inspired these later singers to experiment both tonally and improvisationally. Nevertheless, the overall emotional impression of these early recordings is strong. Although the lyrical content of the songs could vary greatly – some narrating stories of love or tragedy; some dealing with everyday problems of cleaning, cooking and washing; and some very obviously sexually suggestive – the sense one has on listening is that of hearing the sound of a survivor. Despite being called the Blues, these songs use humour and innuendo to suggest a world conquered by those who can best appreciate the simple things in life. The 'unsung' quality described above creates a sometimes conversational, sometimes passionate, and sometimes intimate style that reflects this fundamental theme.

The basic instruments used in early recordings generally employ the most fundamental chord structures in the writing, and melody lines are modest and repetitive. Many of the songs are what one might expect to be written by anyone sitting on their front porch of an evening who had just a rudimentary knowledge of music – and no doubt this is what many of them actually are. This gives an immediate accessibility to the music and a sense that the songs are meant to be both remedial and participatory. They are songs that even a 'non-singer' can feel comfortable with, and lyrically they are filled with the stories of ordinary, straight-talking people who have been through a lot – and survived to tell the tale. A writer like Peter Guralnick (who has devoted an extraordinary amount of writing time on his avowed passion for the Blues) puts this beautifully when he describes the way in which he and his friends were completely enthralled by the form when they first encountered it:

> Blues offered the perfect vehicle for our romanticism. What's more, it offered boundless opportunities for embroidery due to its exotic nature, the vagueness of its associations, and certain characteristics associated with the music itself. For one thing it was an undeniably personal music; whatever the autobiographical truth of the words, each singer doubtlessly conveyed something of himself in his song. Then, too, the lyrics in addition to being poetically abstract, were often vague and difficult to understand; the singer made a habit of slurring syllables or dropping off the end of a verse, and the quality of the recording, often from a distance of thirty-five years, added to the aura of obscurity.[3]

3 Peter Guralnick, *Feel Like Going Home: Portraits in Blues and Rock 'n' Roll* (Edinburgh: Canongate Press, 2003) pp. 22, 23

The fundamental 'authenticity' of adverse experience that marks the Blues as a genre is an effect many singers employ to create a sense of intimacy with the listener and to imply a life experience that has been at once rich, painful and endured with great spirit. The voices may not often be beautiful; rather, they seem to carry the scars of old battles and the weariness of unrelenting toil. But the very fact that they still 'sing' out to us is what gives Blues music such a life-affirming quality. Vocal 'flaws' in this context have meaning and power – it makes little sense to talk about 'improving' or 'fixing' the vocal sounds of Big Mama Thornton or Sonny Boy Williamson, since such unique voices convince us of their honesty.

'GIMME A PIGFOOT AND A BOTTLE OF BEER' – BESSIE SMITH (1933)

Perhaps the best known of the early Blues singers, Bessie Smith's style was no doubt influenced by the need to sing without amplification in large tent shows throughout her early years. In a song like *Gimme a Pigfoot and a Bottle of Beer*, her style can probably best be described as a 'wailed shout'. This is one of Bessie's last recordings and she's a decade into her recording career. At this point she's working with some legendary musicians – Benny Goodman and Jack Teagarden played at these sessions – and she's come a long way from her first recorded hit, *Down Hearted Blues* (1923). If you were to listen to the two recordings together, the first thing you might notice is how much sweeter and more lyrical the early song sounds – even though in many ways she's working with some very similar stylistic choices. *Gimme a Pigfoot and a Bottle of Beer* seems like a vocal illustration of the life of hard drinking Bessie had been leading up to this point. Her predominant vocal qualities are always neutral thick-fold and Belt, with a large share of Rumble sounds thrown in to increase the overall effort-level at the moments she wanted most to emphasise. Her onsets are hard: with an impressive number of Rumble onsets (many voices simply couldn't cope with employing this high-effort effect so often), her diction in the onset is always clean, and never 'eased' into. She doesn't improvise much – although she adds a 'Yeah!' on the piano player verse, which sounds like something beyond her usual Rumble. When you hear her quality on this, you can understand why so many people have described her higher effort-level sounds as a 'growl' – this is definitely growled, and combined with the fall off the note finish, she sounds both dangerous and sexy here. Melodically, this is a very simple tune. Structurally it is just a series of repeated verses, with only one variation, for which Bessie adjusts very quickly up into a thin-fold sound (just slightly flat at one point) and comes right back down onto her comfortable thick-fold/Belt sound. The overall effect is to keep the perceived effort-level of the song consistently very high.

Her note attack here is often a light upward bend, and sustains are mostly pretty brief – indeed, this is one of the things that really distinguishes this track from the earlier *Down Hearted Blues*, where she used much more sustain and vibrato, and also linked her phrases together a bit more elegantly. *Gimme a Pigfoot and a Bottle of Beer* features very little sustain, which means that phrases are often broken at the mid-way point. Where she sustains she never fades – she either compresses her finish quickly without vibrato, or else employs a fairly brief vibrato that finishes with a compressed release, or the occasional fall off the note. Phrase placement is very even, and apart from a little spoken intro, her improvisation is generally confined to her growls. The spoken intro is interesting to listen to, since you can hear how closely her singing voice matches her speaking voice.

Overall, the song adds up to much more than the sum of its relatively simple parts. You can sense that Bessie would have been a great singer to see live. This track doesn't feel like a 'sung' track – she is shouting at you to come and join her. Recording feels a kind of 'cold' medium for her since there's an immediate energy and raunchiness that you feel can't be entirely captured in the studio. In listening, though, you feel in no doubt that she knows what she wants to communicate – she wants to get this party started. She uses her growls, rumbles and shouts to suggest that she's ready to have a good time and wants you to come along. She isn't drinking champagne and it's not a 'champagne' delivery – she's singing about beer, gin and reefers. The rough-and-ready sound of her voice is at once incredibly physical and perhaps this is the greatest impression you get upon hearing her – her voice never comes from her head, it comes from her whole body, once described as 'just this side of voluptuous, buxom and massive, but stately too, shapely as an hour-glass …'.[4] To modern ears, perhaps, this recording now sounds dated and maybe even a bit repetitive, but you can imagine that to a public only just discovering recorded music, this was probably a pleasurably scandalous work.

It was perhaps the overall emotional effect created by her stylistic choices that led to an extraordinary advertisement for one of Bessie's recordings in the 1924 *Chicago Defender*. 'Wow – but Bessie Smith spills fire and fury …

4 Oakley, p. 99

You can almost see hate drip from the piano keys. Fury flies off the violin strings. Every note is a half-note. No quarter for anyone.'[5] Witty as it is, it's unfair – I don't think I hear anything in her recordings that I would associate with 'hate'. But she makes strong choices when she's singing and it leaves you convinced of her own personal strength. And the overall rough-and-ready quality to her singing still nearly defines what it is in Blues singing that appeals to so many.

'TERRAPLANE BLUES' – ROBERT JOHNSON (1936)

Perhaps the most influential Blues artist of all time, Robert Johnson's singing is distinctly different from that of other contemporary Blues singers. Many people see Johnson as the link between early Country Blues and the more urbanised Chicago Blues form. Descriptions like restless, haunting, anxious are commonly applied to his vocal sound and in this track I think you hear all that – but with a powerful measure of joyful defiance thrown in. Johnson was a guitarist of skill and this song works particularly well in the interchange between his singing and playing. You can really hear him attempting to make his voice sound like his guitar playing, especially in his upper register. He was deeply influenced vocally by the way in which he played guitar. He was exceptional in his instrumental exploration and his playing was never heavy-handed or droning, as so many of the Country Blues guitarists were. You almost get the sense that he was impatient with his playing, constantly adding small improvisational pickings where others players would ordinarily just keep a rhythm line steady. He also had a love of the upper range of the instrument and you hear that clearly on this track, where he explores that range continually through quick, high riffs.

Unlike many sung Blues recordings, this song isn't dominated by a single vocal quality – in fact the most arresting thing about it is the quick and interesting changes of vocal qualities. From the high neutral thin-fold sounds of the 'oohs', which 'flip' mid-phrase into Twang sound, to the low-effort neutral thick-fold quality that gives way to the song's only spoken line, he is running through quite a range both in terms of pitch and approach. There is little attempt to shape a phrase, apart from using the melodic arc to create a sense of a rising weight mid-phrase. He uses much note bend throughout. Because of this variety, as well as a wide mix of compressed/falling releases and sustain vibrato fades in neutral thick-fold, the song does very definitely

5 Oakley, p. 101

have a 'sung' feel to it, even if that sung feel is rather thin and pinched at times. But it never sounds schooled, and he never sounds as if he comes fully onto the voice. Perhaps that's what gives his recordings such a jumpy, restless quality. He is bold with his quality changes, which are quick and have an unsophisticated feel to them. He doesn't exploit sustain at all – he uses it when it seems to lead naturally into the guitar break he's planned, and that seems to keep the emotional weight we often associate with sustain at bay.

His lyrics are sexy, couched in an extended metaphor about his 'terraplane', and he sings of raising his woman's 'hood' and tangling with her wires in order to get to her spark plug. Not great literature – but self-consciously not so. As he runs through his metaphor, the range of vocal colour and boldness allows you to feel his joy at the exploration of both his music and his machine.

'DEALING WITH THE DEVIL' – SONNY BOY WILLIAMSON (1940)

Before listening to this track, I wouldn't have thought it possible that one recording could put me in mind so strongly of both Bob Dylan and Mick Jagger at the same time, as these artists' styles differ widely. But this piece by Sonny Boy Williamson does just that. A Blues legend whose career spanned many years, Williamson displays what might be described as a classic male Blues sound here. The diction is very loose – but it isn't really hard to pick up the lyric. Williamson was known to have had a speech impediment, which perhaps influenced the loose diction. As with nearly all Blues, his perfor-mance evokes a very 'spoken' sound and in the middle section of the song he abandons any pretence at singing and just speaks in time – you can hear how closely alike his spoken and sung sounds are. There is really only one vocal quality throughout the song (a neutral thick-fold sound) although you can hear a bit of Creak or 'scratch' overlaid onto that at times.

Williamson was considered one of the early virtuoso Blues harmonica players and his real melodic flights take place in those instrumental solos. The singing has a 'straight' feel to it, as does the whole track, and he weights his phrases quite evenly. He pushes the placement just forwards of the beat in most places, which gives a little sense of forward weighting; but for the most part, the overall effect of evenness adds to the conversational quality of his performance. His note attack is heavily bent in the 'devil' choruses, and instead of the compressed or quick falls off the note that he uses in the verse, he holds onto the end of 'devil' (which he almost pronounces as 'devim') and allows a little fluttery vibrato into a notable bend downwards as the pitch falls off. This particular release reminds you a bit of the sounds he makes later in his harmonica solo. And although the word 'devil' remains heavily weighted throughout the song, that little vibrato and backing off from the full consonant in the end foreshadows his ambivalence about 'dealing' with the devil as the song goes on. In his spoken break he assures us that he's only been a little 'friendly, just friendly' with the devil, and goes on to admit that he 'got in trouble', and that he 'don't do that no more'.

It's a thoroughly playful song, which emphasises joy in survival – the lyrics are a kind of mish-mash of Blues preoccupations: mean, perfidious women, and the hapless men who are taken in by them. But he's not defeated at all – he's ready to find another woman because he refuses to travel this 'big road' by himself. And you know that he finds something life-affirming in the ongoing wars between men and women.

'I JUST WANT TO MAKE LOVE TO YOU' – ETTA JAMES (1960)

It is perhaps not surprising that the decades between the very early recording years and the 1960s wrought so little change in the most basic Blues style, since the overall effect of most Blues music (insofar as one could suggest such a thing!) must be one of authenticity. In this track, Etta James achieves that authenticity though a Blues style that descends directly from Bessie Smith. Listening closely to the recording there is an unmistakable similarity between the two singers.

Etta's vocal power is similar to Bessie Smith's, and has that 'wailed shout' sound – particularly on the verse openings. She uses a neutral thick-fold quality and Belt through most of the song, but allows a kind of 'Aspirate melt' once she gets to lines about making love. You can certainly hear the way in which good sound recording and good microphones have freed singers to really explore the dynamic range of their voices at this point, and Etta goes from a shout to a whisper more than once on this track. Her onsets are where she really concentrates effort-level, constricting right from the very opening. In fact, she uses a lot of Constriction all the way through the song, and this is a great example of how to use that constricted sound to wonderful effect. You can hear that she has fine control of where and when she chooses to use that gritty power, and when she releases into an unconstricted tone the contrast is really satisfying. You can also feel how much more effort-level it takes to create and sustain that Constriction when you compare this sound to Bessie's 'rumbles' and 'growls'. Etta James just pushes the whole physical immediacy of her strength right at you throughout this song. She uses a slow upward bend often in the note attack and her sustains are rare, which keeps the song from sounding too 'sung'. As with most Blues singers, there is little improvisation, and – with the exception of one extended phrase repetition towards the end of the track, and a very few alternative notes – she generally sticks to the melody here. Phrase placement is pretty even, but the hefty constricted openings push all the phrase weight distinctly towards the front. There's little sustain used apart from the big note bends in the first part of some phrases, and most of her finishes are nearly all compressed or falling; this also adds to the sense of all the weight of the phrase being pulled forwards.

Like Bessie, her overall emotional effect is one of great power and passion, and perhaps because the vocal quality changes are a little more intriguing the overall effect of the song is slightly more complex. There's a pure sexual charge here and her quick vocal-quality changes play on both female power and female softness. She sings at one point about wanting to bake her man some bread – but you never get even the slightest hint of anything domestic about Etta James. You know she's just trying to keep his strength up in order to match her own.

'LITTLE RED ROOSTER' – BIG MAMA THORNTON (1968)

An extraordinary song that has been recorded by artists like Sam Cooke, the Rolling Stones, Junior Wells and Howlin' Wolf, this is a truly unique effort, filled with an entire barnyard full of sounds. Big Mama Thornton doesn't so much sing as wail her way through this atmospheric performance. She relies almost entirely on neutral thick-fold and Belt qualities and you can sense the size of her instrument – particularly in the final verse. I wouldn't want to guess exactly what voice qualities she's using for the animal effects! Rather than Rumble, she uses Glottal and (both mildly and heavily) Constricted onsets most frequently, which really ups the perceived effort-level. She does nothing to 'beautify' the sounds she makes – there is relatively little sense of the song being 'sung', and it's filled with the classic kind of defiance that Ma Rainey and Bessie Smith were exhibiting decades earlier. This song was recorded in the 1960s and sound technology has moved on quite a bit. Where Bessie Smith's recording feels almost distant in the hearing, this track has a great sense of immediacy to it.

Big Mama Thornton doesn't build to her final verse – she comes straight in with a powerful Constriction and maintains high-effort voice qualities throughout. Like Etta, she is completely in control of where she employs the constricted sound and also knows how satisfying it is to the listener to hear that Constriction ease into a full and saturated neutral thick-fold or Belt tone. Her note attack is consistently playful – she bends the sound both up and down. She uses little sustain and the quick compressed finishes keep a spoken quality throughout most of the song. Although she includes much more improvisation than does Etta James' song above, she saves most of her improvisational efforts for the animals and the occasional more heavily constricted 'Whoa!'-type sounds. But you feel her strong Gospel roots in the last short improv – strong, and with a downward inflection. She keeps the phrase placement even but always slightly behind the beat. That evenness can feel a bit imposed on Blues songs, since they are so often structured like 'call and response'. Here, she exploits that form playfully with the lead guitarist. She heavily weights the first part of her phrases, and although there is great energy to the animal sounds at the ends of phrases, the finish of the 'sung' phrase tends to feel light as she compresses the finish or else adds a light sustain and very quick vibrato fade. It's a joyful and defiant sound – and certainly *not* a sophisticated one. She refuses to be embarrassed or intimidated by the range of sounds she can make – pleasant and thoroughly unpleasant – and she really explores the lot. Like Smith, Thornton's music is something of a triumph in the battle of the sexes. The song has always been seen as an extended sexual metaphor about a philandering man – although this is anything *but* the sound of a helpless or heartbroken woman. She wants you to know that women can and will survive their wandering men. She's changed the lyric around to fit a woman's perspective — and you certainly get the sense that her 'little bitty' rooster will return.

'AT LAST' – ETTA JAMES (1960)

I've included this song because in many ways it marks the difference between Blues and what we've commonly come to think of as Rhythm & Blues – although this term is somewhat contentious. 'Rhythm & Blues' was coined by *Billboard Magazine* whose editors, by the 1950s, felt that the record industry's use of the term 'race' records for songs recorded by black artists was too close to the term 'racist'. But as James Miller has pointed out, '... the names changed. But the use of racially coded labels remained intact. These labels reflected real musical – and racial – divisions.'[6] For many of the young singers

6 James Miller, *Almost Grown* (London: William Heinemann), 1999, p. 44

I work with, the term R&B is much more familiar to them than Blues, since they can immediately think of an artist who sings R&B but often have difficulty in naming a Blues singer – however familiar they may be with the style. This song by Etta James is a big slushy R&B ballad, and typical of the Blues/Gospel fusion sound of the time – one that has come to be more commonly referred to a 'soul music' or R&B. I think it shares many qualities with the Whitney Houston song we analysed earlier. For me, Etta's great strength still resides in her bolder work (*I Just Want to Make Love to You* or *The Night Time is the Right Time*), but it is interesting to hear her in this crossover sound. In *At Last*, Etta abandons the 'rough and ready' sound of her Bluesier tracks and gets 'artful' – she doesn't deny the beautiful sound she can make, although you can sense that she's quite a bit more at home with the big Belt sound. You can almost imagine that she went into the studio thinking she'd do a nice sugary ballad. But that big old voice just pops out like the return of the repressed. Still, she's worked much harder on shaping the phrases and giving them a more elegant finish than one usually hears in Blues. There are some sustained vibrato fades, which lend this a more elegant feel than a Blues reading might. She still favours weighting the front of the phrase and puts all the big note bends up front. She rarely falls off a note here, and there's much less compression in the note finish than we might hear in her Blues tracks. She's gone for a softer, slightly more 'sung' sound – there's a more 'tilted' quality to the voice, and she eases her way into the first verse with neutral thick-fold sound – rich, deep but not high effort-level for her. She doesn't oversustain, but uses simple, short vibrato fades, then finishes the verse with a big Belt sound. She can never suppress that big Belt for long, but it seems to come so easily to her that you still don't feel she's really working until you get to end of verses. The middle-8 section is surprisingly low-key, until she builds right up into the end and improvs at a higher effort-level. But the song uses much more dynamic variation than any early Blues songs did. You can feel that at this point, artists are getting used to the idea of letting the microphone do a lot of the work for them, so that they can swoop off into these hugely muscular Belts and then come quickly into the microphone for the lighter, airier tones that simply didn't feel available to the early Blues artists.

Perhaps what strikes me most in listening to this 1960s confection of violins and piano triplets is that while the song is about having finally found love 'at last', it utterly lacks the resilience, humour and immediacy of the old Blues sounds. Indeed, the overall effect is one of a kind of melancholy – and if you didn't listen to the words you probably wouldn't distinguish this from a kind of 'heartbreak' ballad. It may just be my own prejudice, but I definitely prefer Etta in her harder 'Blues' mode doing *I Just Want to Make Love to You* recorded on the same album.

SUMMARY

Blues singers from Memphis Minnie to Muddy Waters have always given the listener an almost voyeuristically personal experience of sharing the singer's pain and their ultimate survival. It's a form that really champions equality of the sexes – both men and women survive here with strength and style. The 'basics' of early Blues vocal sound include:

1. A downward inflection in the vocal delivery that almost imitates the downward inflection of someone wailing or crying.
2. An 'unsung' sound that is achieved largely though the use of thick-fold and sometimes Belt qualities that give a close-to-spoken feel about the voice.
3. Effort-levels used by Blues singers vary dramatically. For the women the effort-level is usually very high, largely owing to the predominant use of Belt, Twang and neutral thick-fold voice qualities. For the men – most of whom played instruments while singing – the effort-levels were not always so high and in most cases remained closer to medium level since they most often employed neutral thick-fold qualities. There are, of course, many exceptions to this (Howlin' Wolf comes to mind).
4. A tendency to fall off the note – a part of the downward pattern of inflection noted above – with either little or no vibrato, or else to compress finishes to give a more 'spoken' sound.
5. Little build or improvisation in the sustain.
6. Even phrase placement, and often a tendency to weight the beginnings of phrases.
7. Frequent upward or downward bend in the note attack.
8. Little attempt to 'beautify' the sound of the tone – a kind of 'rough and ready' feel to the delivery.
9. Inconsistent diction, sometimes mumbled delivery.

PRACTICE

These general elements of Blues style are not as evident in this 'pure' form today as they once were, but learning to work with them can help to free you as a vocalist from some of the limitations we place on ourselves when we're singing for someone else's approval. You'll find this exercise a lot more effective if you can work with a tape recorder – it doesn't have to be of great quality. Find a song that fits comfortably into your neutral thick-fold range. Ideally, you might know a Blues song that you could use for this exercise, although the traditional spiritual songs I've used in examples so far work really well for all the style exercises, so you might want to use one of them. Remember – you can use tracks 23 and 25 on the Demo CD if you want to try this exercise with *Swing Low, Sweet Chariot*.

1. Sing your song through once, concentrating on what you want to communicate with it. Don't worry about anything technical – just concentrate on communicating something important (perhaps just in terms of where the song feels most emotionally 'connected' to you?).

2. Now that you've worked the song through once, try again. This time – particularly in those areas of the song with which you feel the strongest connection – see what happens if you concentrate on using the highest effort-level voice quality you can. You may find it easier to Belt, 'wail', or 'shout' if you move the song up a little in your comfortable range. Resist the urge to sustain notes, and when you come to the ends of phrases, either compress your finishes or fall off the notes. These finishes can feel really unnatural if you've not used them before. Listen back to your performance – it may not 'sound' like you, but it's bound to have a different sound from your first attempt.

3. If there was anything you liked in that performance – even if only your own bravery! – hang onto it and try again. This time, maintain a thick-fold quality in the singing, but see whether you can add weight to the beginning of phrases – either with hard glottal onsets, slightly rumbled or slightly constricted onsets, and some bend in the note attack. Let the diction slide a bit, especially towards the ends of phrases. If you can, try also to keep in mind what it was that you made your strongest emotional connection to – it will help to keep these exercises from being too mechanical.

4. Finally, choose a Blues artist whose style you really like. Spend some time analysing their work (much in the same way that we did with the Whitney Houston song). Notice what they do with voice qualities, onsets, tone releases, phrase placement, diction, improv, effort-levels, etc. Now find a song that your artist has *not* recorded, and attempt to do the song 'in the style of' your artist. This isn't a *Stars in Their Eyes* kind of effort – you're not trying to *sound* like the artist, but rather trying out the elements of style that you think really mark their performances.

If some of this comes easy to you, and you liked the roughness and the immediacy of your sound, you're probably a Blues 'natural'! If you couldn't really stop laughing – well, don't give up. You may not see yourself as a Blues singer or you may find this style too demanding/foreign. It will help you to do more listening in this style because it gives you real freedom in terms of making sounds that *aren't* correct or beautiful – and that calls for a bit of bravado on your part. The more you listen, the more you'll learn to appreciate the humour, strength, and generosity of Blues singing.

Gospel

Gospel is the great Mother, the church a repository of women's memory, nurture, liberation and catharsis. Its moral codes may be strict, but it is a place where women feel safe in a full expression of self. When [Aretha] Franklin's father, the Reverend C.L., who in the mid '50s could command up to $4,000 fees for an appearance on the Gospel circuit, let loose his million-dollar roar, working women would surrender themselves to ecstatic prayer, some having to be carried away by strong-armed nurses.[7]

Gospel is closely allied with Blues in the sense of its strong roots in black American history and experience, and also in its overall sound and the vocal choices made by Gospel singers. There are many styles that seem to operate under the category of Gospel, and singers as diverse as Aretha Franklin, Elvis Presley and Louis Armstrong have recorded Gospel songs or albums. Gospel

7 Lucy O'Brien, *She-Bop* (London: Penguin Books), 1995, p. 86

is also, of course, a group style – from quartet to choir – and the range of sounds in these groups moves from highly syncopated and rhythmic almost 'barbershop-style' close harmonies to the fuller, more traditional sounds of liturgical choir music sung in response.

Gospel as a movement has mutated greatly from its earliest manifestations in the crossover between the field 'spiritual' and the Southern church 'witnesses'. Early Gospel stars were highly celebrated by their audiences as they travelled the 'Gospel Highway' circuit, and they worked in various group/solo combinations. It is generally held that the first great 'crossover' artist from Gospel to popular, secular 'chart' music was Sam Cooke – and although his was certainly the success which had greatest impact, there were others whose 'crossover' attempts preceded his. Cooke's impact inspired many other Gospel singers to take the high-risk gamble of crossing over into secular music – and it was indeed high-risk, as the Gospel community could be very unforgiving of such a choice. This crossover Gospel sound is often referred to as Soul music or R&B, and it is distinct from Blues in a number of general ways. But of course, the links between these sounds are obvious as well. Contemporary Gospel recordings – such as those by the Harlem Gospel Choir and the London Community Gospel Choir – are barely distinct from contemporary Rhythm & Blues recordings, either in their instrumentation or in the overall sound of the repertoire.

The sound of a Gospel soloist is one that also varies widely, but perhaps the most identifiable Gospel solo quality is a big Belting sound. And although some of these Belts can be quite Twangy at the top end, they often maintain a very 'chesty' Belt sound. Gospel style is also associated with wide sweeps up to the note, and a kind of 'hollering' style in the improvisation. There is less reliance on the downward inflection of Blues, and much more upward bend in the note, as if trying to suggest through song, the way to heaven. Gospel does not tend to imitate the sound of crying in the sense that Blues singing sometimes does, but can have the 'wail' of an impromptu church response like 'Amen, brother!'.

Very early Gospel singers were working acoustically and often singing above a large church choir. It is possible, perhaps, that the call and response sound of many Gospel numbers originated from the early call and response of church liturgy. But it seems just as likely that the call and response was a way of allowing the solo voice some audibility against the large choir. Perhaps also the tendency to wail and improv on notes in the highest part of the singer's range was similarly an attempt to cut through the sound of the choir and be heard. Metaphorically, of course, the high wailing style of some Gospel singers seems to reach right up to God.

There is a physicality and muscularity to Gospel singing that seems to attest to the depths of a singer's belief. Strong and rich, that belief seems to need to permeate the singer's body as if overtaken by the 'holy spirit'. Perhaps this leads to a kind of freedom for the vocalist, since all sounds made in this context must be holy; and perhaps that's why some of the improvisation is so free and exuberant. Indeed, Gospel granted a kind of extraordinary licence in both its artists and its audience – complete abandon and expression of passion was licensed in this spiritual sphere. This tradition of wails, shouts, moans and utter ecstasy occurring within the sanctified church realm was no doubt the reason that so many within the Gospel audience turned their backs so completely upon those artists who stopped 'singing for God' and started singing 'for the world'. It must have felt like a betrayal, and an act of sacrilege.

Gospel music has many vocal ensemble forms – some in more traditional choir mode, some of them quite at home next to contemporary R&B groups. Some of the older, smaller groups, like the Golden Gate Quartet or the Heavenly Gospel Singers, are most distinguished through the close, syncopated style of the harmonies, which became a clear forerunner of so many of the early R&B, Motown and '50s rock groups. A singer like Sam Cooke, while pure Gospel, was remarkable for the way in which his uniquely smooth, sandy tone almost belied the high effort he put into so many of his performances. But for most people, it's the female Gospel solo – with its extended melismatic displays and sheer power – that has come to define the style. Lucy O'Brien's analysis, quoted above, perhaps explains why, for many, it is the women Gospel soloists who have always captured something particularly extraordinary in this form and proved the most popular of the Gospel artists.

Very early recordings of Gospel singers suggest that they were clearly influenced by the style of their Blues and Jazz-singing sisters. Listening to Sister Rosetta Tharpe now is an interesting experience, because she is capable both of the raw Blues 'shout' in her work, and also has a more artful sound in most of her singing – some of the later recordings sound remarkably like the young Ella Fitzgerald. She was capable of a wide range of stylistic elements and these, along with the dominance of Belt quality in her performances, raises the perceived effort-level of the songs. Songs like *Rock Daniel* or *God Don't Like It* both draw on a number of Blues techniques, including high effort-level onsets like Rumble and Constriction, and a 'shouted' sound combined with a downward inflection at the ends of phrases.

Overall, the songs sit in a higher register than many Blues songs, and while there is more improvisation than in most Blues recordings of the time, they remain relatively modest by contemporary standards.

'HIS EYE IS ON THE SPARROW' – FIVE BLIND BOYS OF MISSISSIPPI (1964)

This is a really fantastic track for illustrating what makes the Gospel sound so unique. The lead vocal is combined with a kind of short sermon, and the whole recording demonstrates clearly the connection between the preaching and the singing sounds of a Gospel church service. The first full minute of the track is spoken, and there is another spoken break mid-way through the song that continues the inspirational storyline. And of course, it's a story about the way in which we can seek comfort through the strength of our spiritual belief. The opening part of the sermon is delivered in a fairly relaxed, if beautifully resonant, spoken voice, and the rich sound of the voice seems to continue quite naturally into the very 'schooled' and beautiful sound of the singing voice in these first few lines. With just solo voice and piano, we can hear how the play of improvisation and extension between these two really are at the heart of this kind of solo Gospel delivery.

Gospel thrives on short, isolated phrasing. Rather than pursuing a sense of melodic 'line' through a song, Gospel artists tend to chop phrases (sometimes even single words) into small parts and dwell upon them either through improvisation or through lengthy sustain. Here is a part of the broken pattern of this version of *His Eye is on the Sparrow*:

Why should my heart // feel lonely //
and long // for heaven // and home
When Je // sus is // my portion //
a con // stant // friend // is he //
His eye // is on // the sparrow //
And I know // He watches // me

There are a lot of unexpected breaks in the words or phrases – certainly not adding up to a sense of a sung-through 'line', which is highly valued in Classical singing style. But in between all of these small broken phrases you can hear the play of the piano, which is mirroring the vocal with a series of similarly broken chord arpeggios running up the scale. There's a wonderful moment in the spoken part in the middle of the track, where the bold and passionate sounds of a proselytising preacher lead to a bit of Constriction and very high effort-level in the speaking voice, and that is matched once the singing comes back in. There is most definitely a 'sung' feeling here, and along with a lot of sustain in the short phrases, there is much variety in the vocal colour – we hear Belt, neutral thick-fold and even some delicate thin-fold sounds (especially on the final 'sparrow' lyric), combined with a beautiful fluttery vibrato sustain that fades gently. But the great majority of the finishes are compressed in just the same way as the piano player quickly stops between phrases, or else fall quickly off the note. There are many short improvisational extensions – rarely more than three or four notes at a time, and very definite heavy upward bend in the note attack. It's difficult to talk about phrase placement, because this kind of Gospel style always feels 'out of time'. The vocalist and piano player sort of follow each other, and where most tracks of this kind usually come into some kind of rhythmic groove, this one stays thoroughly out of time all the way through – a fairly common technique in Gospel solo singing. It's an incredibly uplifting and fascinating recording that convinces you that it's being delivered with unshakeable conviction and great physical commitment.

'PRECIOUS LORD (TAKE MY HAND)' – ARETHA FRANKLIN (1956)

Perhaps nothing comes closer to defining what most contemporary singers have come to think of as Gospel style than the recordings made of 14-year-old Aretha Franklin in 1956, as she sang live in her father's New Bethel Baptist Church in Detroit. The recording is far from perfect, but the passion is unmistakable. It's difficult to attempt to render a musical notation of what the young Aretha does with a Gospel standard like *Precious Lord (Take My Hand)*; for our purposes here, I think it might be more instructive to try yet another kind of graphic notation – one that simply looks at the way in which the lyric carries the weight of the vocal style. Here is the first verse of the hymn:

Precious Lord, take my hand
Lead me on, let me stand
When my way grows drear
Precious Lord linger near
When my light is almost gone
Hear my cry, hear my call
Hold my hand lest I fall
Take my hand precious Lord, lead me home

I want to attempt a kind of rough graphic depiction of the way in which the highly complicated improvisational patterns that Aretha uses in her performance actually lie within the phrases – and you will see the familiar small, isolated chunks of phrasing. Each repeated vowel represents an added note, and each bold letter (roughly!) indicates a heavy upward bend in the note attack:

Leeead
leeead
le**a**d me **o**oooon
To the l**i**ight (wh**ooo**ooa)
take my h**aa**and
Preci**oo**ous **lo**ooooooord
and l**e**ad
y**ou**r chi**ii**iild **o**oon home
When m**ii**y
when my way gro**ooo**oows drear
Pree precious l**oo**ooord
pl**e**eease linger near
And **oo**ooooo when m**y**yy when my light
iii**ii**is al**mo**ooooooost al
moooooost almost g**oo**one
Father, f**aaa**ath**e**eeeer
father hear my pr**a**yer looord
and **oo**h hear my caaaall
And h**o**ooooold hold myyy h**o**ld m**y** h**a**aaand
peace of jesus
l**e**st **I** f**a**all wh**oo**o
Take my haaand,
pr**e**eeci**o**us l**o**ooooord
and l**ee**ad
m**e**eeeee
l**e**ad me h**o**ooome.

No doubt this is a strange way to look at a singing performance – but it serves to demonstrate something about the Gospel style that is difficult to explain in any other way. This is the way in which the isolated Gospel phrases are both extended and weighted: here, you can literally see the way in which this classic performance isolates and then weights those small phrases very heavily towards the front and the middle. As you look through, you can see that although there are some 'weighty' phrase finishes in terms of improvisation, they don't tend to feel heavy in the listening because the massive upward swoop in the preceding note attack tends to throw the emphasis squarely onto the first part of the word. Stylistically, phrase weight and note attack are the most distinctive things about such big, Belting Gospel performances. The dominant vocal quality here is Belt, with Twang on the really high notes. Most onsets are Simultaneous or Glottal, and tone release is gentle, sometimes with final consonants unvoiced. The perceived effort-level is extremely high throughout the song – even from the very start – and the true effort-level is likely to be as high as the perceived one.

The emotional quality of the performance is undeniable – and although for many it may simply all be too much, there's no doubting the passionate spiritual quality of the performance. And perhaps this is one of Gospel's enduring traits. While it takes great technique and artistry to perform it well, it does, at its most basic level, seem to want to deny any sense of 'art' insofar as 'art' may be linked to anything artificial. This particular recording is 'flawed' at many points; there are moments of wayward pitching and at times Franklin's voice fails altogether. But – as is so often the case with emotionally charged, raw performances of popular music — it is doubtful that any Gospel aficionado would want to see these 'flaws' fixed.

'AMAZING GRACE' – MAHALIA JACKSON

Many consider Mahalia Jackson the sort of 'godmother' of all Gospel singers and her sound is very different from Franklin's – although this is largely an effect of overall tonal quality. Her dominant vocal quality is Belt, but she has a very 'dark' sound in the Belt which feels as if she's mixing it with Elongated quality at the lower end. In mid-range she's producing a pure Belt, which naturally has a very dark timbre. It gives a great resonance to the sound. It is a very powerful voice and the overall Elongated feel of the tone lends both significance and a real dignity to her performances.

Although the differences between the two singers feels strong in the listening, I've come to see how similar they are in terms of their basic style choices – and it is this which leads me to think that the difference felt is largely one of vocal quality. Below I've taken a small fragment of a live recording of *Amazing Grace* and I've done a similar graphic analysis to the one on *Precious Lord*:

Aaaamaz iiiiiiing Grace
Hooooow // Sweeeeet
theee // soound
Thaaat // saved
aaaaaa // wreeeetch
liiiike mee
liii once
waas loooooost
huuut noow // lii'm foound
Waaas blind // buut noooooooow
liiiii caannnn see.

I've found this rather unusual method helpful when listening closely to performances of such overwhelming power and improvisational flight, and I think these graphic representations make clear how, despite the very different tone qualities between Aretha Franklin and Mahalia Jackson, the fundamental choices they make about phrase placement and phrase weight are very similar. It seems that Mahalia is less inclined to break the phrases into the smaller chunks that Aretha does, although this is extremely hard to judge when listening to her sing. What she does tend to do is treat each word almost as a separate unit in itself. There is very little sense of 'flow' in the sung line. She places the weight mid-word with much bend coming into the vowel that she's about to improvise around, and in the section shown above there are only two points ('wretch like ME' and 'can SEE') at which she sustains an end of phrase. All other tone releases are compressed (with one pushed release), and many of the final consonants are either unvoiced or very softly voiced.

SUMMARY
The overall impression is that each word has great weight within the overall performance, and the power and solemnity of Mahalia Jackson's tone give this performance a truly 'church'-like atmosphere. The improvisation here is neither as spontaneous nor as (occasionally) wayward as the young Aretha Franklin's, but for all their differences, both artists exemplify what I believe is still at the heart of the Gospel solo singing genre:

1   Vocal qualities dominated by Belt and Twang.
2   A heavy reliance on upward bend in note attack and extended sustain.
3.   A tendency to break phrases into small chunks, and to weight the phrases

very heavily towards the front or the middle; less tendency to sustain in phrase endings.

4. Little sense of 'flow' in the performance.

5. An extremely melismatic approach, often concentrating improvisation mid-word, rather than at phrase endings. Very high effort-levels – both perceived and true.

PRACTICE

We'll use *'Swing Low, Sweet Chariot'*. You'll want to be somewhere *very* soundproof, or else home alone, so you can make mistakes without worrying about how you'll sound! Try the verse through first in a range that allows you to use a lot of Belt and Twang voice qualities, if you can access those easily:

If you get to Heaven before I do
Comin' for to carry me home
Tell all my friends I'm comin' there too
Comin' for to carry me home

Next, try the following, and make sure you find a different note for every vowel you see here:

Iiif yoou get to heeeaven
Before Iiiii dooo
Comin' foor to carry meeeee hooooome
Tell aaaall my frieeends
I'm comin' there tooooo
Comin' for to caaaary meeeeeee hoooooome

Make sure you're not allowing a sense of 'flow' as you sing – break the phrases up into bits. Now try this through once more, adding a few very hefty bends in the note attacks – perhaps on the words 'you', 'home' and 'all'.

It's probably sounding pretty mechanical (and not a little weird) – but go through a few times (and feel free to drop or add a few notes when you want to). For reasons I can't wholly explain, my students have always found this exercise easier to do when approaching it in this way, than when asked to just try doing long extended melodic improvisations spun out of their own imaginings. It may be that concentrating so hard on figuring out how many vowels/notes there are releases some of their self-consciousness. Even if this feels quite difficult for you, or if you have a very hard time finding enough improvised notes, with a little practice you can really start to get the feel of this style, so it's worth sticking at it.

Make sure you keep the weight of the phrases towards the front. Don't always hang onto your sustain at the end of each phrase – allow long improvs in the middle to take that work from you. There's a lot of sustain in Gospel, but quite a lot of it tends to happen mid-phrase. And remember that Gospel style doesn't really flow – it's very 'chopped up' and the weight usually occurs within individual words. If any of this comes easily to you, you're probably a Gospel 'natural'! If it doesn't, spending some time really listening and then trying things out will pay off in terms of increasing your confidence with R&B/Soul as well as Gospel sounds – and the joy in being able to do this kind of music well is pretty indescribable!

Jazz

Jazz exists (and came to exist) through tensions, which ultimately became syntheses – all of which give it the strangely indefinable character that makes analysis so challenging. These tensions – which came to sit alongside one another – are between Black/White (the European musical traditions vs. non-European, African-American sound); Hot/Cool (the sometimes wild and reckless solo sounds vs. the cool, urbane musical sophistication); Heart/ Head (free expressive instincts and untrained musicians vs. a structured and profound musical knowledge); and Raw/Refined (growling, rasping, passionate noises vs. a purer aesthetic with regard to timbre). Because Jazz began first as an instrumental form, Jazz singing seemed to have to search to find its form in a sense. It wasn't, like Blues, just a matter of allowing the heart to lead. Jazz musical form was fairly sophisticated even in its early years, following on from Ragtime and March music and involving instruments that required a higher degree of musical knowledge to play than the guitar/ banjo/harmonica instrumentations so familiar in Blues form.

The early influential Jazz orchestra leaders (Fletcher Henderson, Duke Ellington) were well-educated artists, whose musical skills brought significant changes to the form. It was *not* a vocal form in its infancy and many of the vocal performances recorded with Jazz bands in the '20s/'30s drew heavily on Blues form – but this wasn't an entirely happy marriage. The Blues form was in many ways dominated by the vocal performance. As an instrumental form, Jazz singers often had to take the part of the 'straight man' – they were left to sing the melody while all around them erupted spontaneous instrumental flights around and away from the melody. Still, the singers couldn't be *too* straight with the melody, or they would inhibit the 'swing' sound of Jazz. People often think that Jazz singing has to include extended improvisational skills, which can make it seem as if the form is rather ornate. But in truth, the great Jazz singers often did quite the opposite: they reduced and simplified as often as – if not more often than – they embellished. Billie Holiday's great influence was in her ability to simplify a melody line – often allowing some tension or dissonance between the sung line and the harmonic changes beneath the singing. Those tensions had a 'blue' sound and along with this she employed a kind of 'wayward' style in the note attack. This is the smallest kind of improvisation – just a very fast rise and fall in pitch sound before settling on to the note. Like many other 'cool' Jazz singers she brings a truly unique tonal quality and a profoundly unusual ability to phrase against the expected ground beat. It is a subtle but very skilled playfulness.

Early distinctions between European tradition and Blues could be heard in the voices of Armstrong and Holiday – particularly in the desire to deviate from the European standards of 'timbre'. Early Jazz instrumentalists often went to extreme lengths to adjust the sounds of their instruments – modifying pianos so that they lost their 'concert' purity, or finding various ways to mute or change the sound of instruments like the trumpet. These same desires can be heard in some of the unusual sounds of some of the singers. In a way they also typify a split that might be characterised as the 'hot' or 'cool' sound of Jazz vocalists – the 'hotter' sound working perceptively harder in effort-level and generally using the voice as a band instrument. The 'cool' sound often brought beauty of tone to market, and lent a kind of 'silken', floating feel to the melody – which was always creatively (rather than 'accurately') placed, allowing a 'swing' Jazz feel to a track.

Absolutely no one is comfortable trying to define Jazz, although a number of people would insist that there are defining factors which unite all of its disparate camps: syncopation and improvisation. As I must talk in general terms here, for the singer, I would suggest that there are perhaps some identifiable traits in Jazz singing, although of course there are no 'rules'.

Technical changes allowed much more subtlety in the choices available to the early Jazz singers. Where many of the Blues artists had sung in an acoustic setting in tent shows and small theatres, the widespread use of microphones changed the vocalists' point of concentration. Now no longer worried about having to 'sing over' the accompaniment to be heard, there were any number of subtler and more varied choices available to singers, and perhaps key amongst them was the ability to employ the quieter vocal qualities – thinfold, Aspirate, Elongated.

Perhaps more than any other form we'll look at here, there seems to me a strong sense of distinctions in Jazz style – nowhere better heard than in a classic track called *Now You Has Jazz*, sung by Bing Crosby and Louis Armstrong. Crosby's style – a smooth, elegant, aloof and even, arguably, ironic sound – is a classic example of the sophisticated Jazz singer; he is a man possessed of much vocal power and musicality but his expression is somehow intellectualised and cool. Armstrong's style, on the other hand, is immediate, sensuous, unconcerned with 'beauty' of tone, and seems to admit little difference between the notion of the voice as the bearer of a lyrical tale and the voice as an instrument like any other in the band – not surprisingly, here, a trumpet. His exuberant bursts of improvisation Rumble, Creak and bleat, and it is fitting that the lyric he sings is about 'le Jazz hot', since compared to Crosby his style is a hotter, wilder sound.

Overall, Jazz stylists always tended to value (and want their listeners to value) musical skill, and the ability to extend harmonic territory. Quite opposed to the 'rough and ready' similarity found in the tonal quality of many Blues singers, nearly every great Jazz singer has displayed an arguably distinctive sound to the voice. That distinction may lie in the very smooth and somewhat 'sandy' tones of 'cooler' artists like Ella Fitzgerald, Mel Torme, June Christy, Nat King Cole or Norah Jones, or in the utterly unique tonal qualities as well as the range of complementary elements employed by 'hotter' Jazz singers like Dinah Washington, Sarah Vaughan, Nancy Wilson, or Al Jarreau. All these singers share certain musical attributes, chief amongst which must be the accuracy and confidence of their pitching.

Like the earlier Blues songs and artists, early Jazz singers like Billie Holiday and Mildred Bailey sang the songs of people who had been through difficulties and survived, but the sweeter quality and more complex stylistic elements used by these singers suggested a kind of fragility or vulnerability that many people find emotionally charged. In the case of an artist like Billie Holiday, the personal tragedies seem to blend almost imperceptibly into the haunting, searching sounds she creates on a song like *Strange Fruit*.

As the form evolved, however, the sense of deep emotional involvement with the material has often been happily traded for the pursuit of technical excellence. This kind of great technical skill in many cases has meant that the vocalist abandoned lyrics altogether to compete outright with instrumental soloists through 'scat' singing – the emotional effect of which is not generally profound. Nevertheless, the power of such vocal wizardry is strong, and the overall effect of hearing such vocal confidence is often simple wonder at such virtuosity.

This makes the idea of Jazz singing one that intimidates many singers, who have come to feel that the foremost requirement of such singing is extended improvisational technique. A quick glance at the history of Jazz singing, however, doesn't necessarily bear this out: singers like Tony Bennett and Dinah Washington are less impressive for their 'virtuosity' than for their unique tone and risky stylistic choices. Peggy Lee and June Christy were singers of the 'cool' Jazz variety and although the accuracy of their pitching is pretty breathtaking, they relied heavily on their beauty of tone.

The emotional effect of Jazz singing almost certainly varies with each individual artist, and with the highly complex experience that individual listeners bring to the music. But it isn't too contentious to propose that Jazz singing is overall a 'cooler' medium than Blues or Gospel, and that in Jazz it generally isn't raw, authentic life experience that we're after. Jazz is a more self-consciously art-for-art's-sake style, and it's doubtful that anyone felt greatly in touch with the pain of the black American experience when listening to Ella Fitzgerald's 1938 hit *A-Tisket A-Tasket*. Instead, they heard a joyful if not profound sound that appealed by virtue of its ability to sustain a tension between the cool and worldly sound of the musicians and the childishly simple subject matter of the song.

Jazz appeals to an urban ideal: the dream of sophisticated city living. To that end the kind of raw emotional connection with material that is common to Blues or Gospel is deliberately avoided. There is little to comprehend, emotionally, from Nina Simone's absolute certainty in *My Baby Just Cares for Me*, other than mere mortal appreciation of her supreme confidence. It is a life-affirming sound that proposes music as the joyful expression of reason – and in its more progressive forms an almost mathematically precise reason mastered and rendered unique in the solos of musical virtuosos.

So how does the Jazz singer achieve this more reasoned, less emotional sound? Overall I think Jazz singers tend to see less distinction between the voice and any other instrument in the band. To that end, then, there is often more attention given to diction and the sound of lyrics generally. This is less to do with 'telling the story of the song' than with actually employing consonants and vowels in the way that an instrumentalist concentrates on the various components which make up his/her sound. There is often much more sense of play between vocalist and instrumentalist. And as Jazz instrumentalists became increasingly concerned with the purity of the tone they could coax from their instruments, similarly, Jazz vocalists seemed to reflect their concern with achieving a kind of purity of tone. Perhaps something like Peggy Lee's *Fever* comes closest to exemplifying some of these ideas. The play between voice and percussion on the oft-repeated lyric 'Fever!', which is never really 'sung' in any sense; the minimalism of the vocal performance against the overall minimalism of the production; these are good examples of the way in which Jazz, as a medium, seems to want to find better, more interesting ways to incorporate the human voice as instrument with other instruments in an ensemble.

Improvisation is part of Jazz singing, and it is here that the voice-as-instrument approach is important. Of course, one of the greatest differences between the voice and most other instruments is that you don't have valves or keys on a keyboard to help fix a pitch. Vocal pitching is a fairly mysterious process in which we simply 'know' where to place a sound. In Jazz singing improvisation is more complex than standard Blues or Gospel vocal riffs. There can be difficult patterns to the improvisation, and sometimes those patterns can feel more 'instrumental' than vocal. In other words, where many vocalists feel safest improvising around a range of notes within a comfortable proximity of one another, Jazz vocalists like Ella Fitzgerald or Al Jarreau can sometimes dazzle with the unexpected – in perhaps the same way that a keyboard player can move as easily from one note to a minor third as s/he can from that same note to an octave or more away. There is often more experimentation in phrase weight and placement, and again this may be related to a more 'instrumental' approach to vocal solos.

'YOU RASCAL YOU' – LOUIS ARMSTRONG (1931)

Although I have tried to keep all the songs used for analysis in this book easily locatable on iTunes, I had to make an exception for the Mahalia Jackson track, and for Louis Armstrong's *You Rascal You*. You can download versions of this song from iTunes, and there is an early version available, but the recording quality isn't great. The recording I'm analysing here only seems to be available on CD. I love this track – it gives us a great chance to hear the whole spectrum of sound that Armstrong can make, and it really makes clear why so many people see him as the first great Jazz singer. He talks through the opening, and in the end, and you can hear that in his speaking – as in his singing – he has real control over how much 'rumbled' sound he makes. The whole of the piece has a spoken quality; he uses the same sounds in speech as in the singing voice.

It's a song that really builds in terms of looseness and swing, and in keeping with that, Armstrong's diction gets fuzzier as the song goes on. As with his horn playing, he approaches song with great freedom and his improvisation pattern as a vocalist very clearly imitates his horn improvisation. He brings a nice easy bend to the note attack, but there is no real 'sung' sound here, which means that his vocal improvisation has a highly percussive sound – he clearly enjoys singing in the way in which he plays his horn. He sings and plays in and around the beat, often lagging just behind or playfully pushing the phrase forwards of the beat, and towards the end there is a great, syncopated play between his vocal and the rhythm section. He draws a lot on the Blues styles of the time in his 'rough-and-ready' vocal delivery, and his phrase weight relies on a kind of rising weight towards the middle, which falls away towards the end of lines. But you can really hear the influence of the Jazz music of the time too – the melodic range here is just so impressive. He uses a lot of his trademark 'rumble' sound, but also in the early part of the song uses a speech quality – even when he's not 'rumbling' there's a lot of air/huskiness in the tone. He begins the piece by talking about how happy he'll be when the rascal he's singing about is dead, but it's a very funny song and uses some outrageous sounds to exaggerate the humour (presumably you can't get away with singing about how happy you'll be when someone dies unless you *do* introduce humour!). He has great confidence in the 'blue' notes, which can sometimes sound as if he veers on the flat side but always reach the pitch he's aiming for. Like so much of Armstrong's output, this is an experience of absolute joy and proves that even when he's talking about death he can't help but affirm the great pleasure of life.

Trying to judge the effort-level here is a challenge. The heaviness of the vocal quality and the exploration of range should lead it towards the high end of perceived effort in listening, but in a manner typical of Jazz, the ease of his reading, the lack of sustain, the overall 'relaxed' approach to singing (he clearly doesn't care about sounding beautiful or correct!), the laughter, and the way in which he seems to just bounce so easily over the ground beat makes it feel almost effortless.

'THE MIDNIGHT SUN' (1964) AND 'LADY BE GOOD' (1947) - ELLA FITZGERALD

The Midnight Sun is a beautiful and rather gentle track from the great lady of Jazz, and I've included it here largely because some of her bigger flights of improvisation and musical imagination can be a bit intimidating. Legendary Jazz vibes player Lionel Hampton and Big Band leader Sonny Burke originally wrote *The Midnight Sun*, and like most Jazz instrumental melodies it has a beautifully catchy but very complex structure. This makes it fairly difficult even for a virtuoso scat/improvisation artist like Ella Fitzgerald to take the piece too far afield, and for that reason it's really interesting to look closely at what she does with it.

She never pushes the effort-level at all – she stays very comfortably within her neutral thin- and thick-fold tones with only some slight shadings of Aspirate sounds on the upper end of the first lines in every verse, and a hint of Elongated quality as she gets towards the lower end of the register in the last lines of the verse. Her onsets and releases are not highly varied – she consistently uses Simultaneous or very soft Glottal onsets. Releases are predominantly vibrato fades, and these things combined give a very smooth and 'sung' sound. Her tone is beautiful, if not passionate, and her pitching is, of course, remarkably accurate. What is interesting in her interpretation here is the way in which she manipulates the phrases very gently to allow herself some 'breathing' room within them. This is a particularly 'wordy' piece with an extraordinary lyric. It is said that Mercer heard the original instrumental version on the radio while driving along the coast in California and that he composed it all in his head then. Whatever the truth of this legend, you certainly feel that Mercer was pushing poetic lyric form quite hard with some pretty spectacular results (even the 'chalice/palace/borealis' rhyme of the first verse is so impressive), and along with a very evenly placed and constantly moving descending melody line, the singer needs to stay pretty closely near the melody as written. Ella gets around this very neatly – nearly every phrase is placed just forwards of the beat. This gives her time to linger now and then on the lyrics mid-phrase, either stretching them just gently beyond their natural 'fall' within the line (thus allowing her to play and swing around the beat easily), or else giving her time to dwell on the very small melodic variations she adds in the first full sing-through of the song. After the instrumental break she comes back in with a much bolder deviation from the melody throughout the whole of the last repeat verse and chorus. It's such a highly structured melody that she has to be pretty careful in the way that she reinvents it, but she does certainly reinvent it for the first two lines coming in, throughout which she only hits two notes as written. She doesn't stray quite as far thereafter — often only jumping up four or five tones on a single note and dropping quickly back into the standard melody line. The overall effect is one of sheer effortless musicality and gentle beauty — a very 'cool' Jazz sound.

It's interesting to contrast this with her 'hotter' approach in Lady Be Good. Here she works very differently in this George and Ira Gershwin classic. Although she 'scats' and invents all around the track, she actually compresses the written melody line within the verse. Instead of singing it through the way that it is actually written, she flattens a fairly rangy melody in the first few verse lines by centering on one note and playing gently around that central note through the line until the end. She adds extensive improvisation at the ends of lines and adds both notes and words in between the written verse lines. The track starts with a great sense of energy and you can almost feel that she is just allowing herself to warm up gently on the first two verses and middle-8 before she takes off for full flight as an 'instrumental' soloist midway through. She allows herself extraordinary play in the sounds she makes here — and instead of the usual remarkable consistency of sung sound that we usually get when she is singing lyric (very consistent neutral thin- or thick-fold sounds, vibrato fades, easy onsets), we get much more compression in the finish, harder glottals and consonants, more falls off the note, and much wilder sounds. At one point she adds extended Creak or 'scratch' into the tone, which is quite rare for her. But you know that she's imitating sounds of other instrumental soloists (like Louis Armstrong) who brought a kind of gritty tonal colour to their instruments and had great influence on Jazz vocalists. For me, these grittier, more exciting sounds really bring her voice to life. The improvisation on this track is both inspiring and incredible and reminds us just why she is considered the finest Jazz vocalist of all time. She had a remarkable command of musical structure and it isn't surprising that when Chick Webb (who was the leader of the first band Ella joined when she was a young woman) died, Ella led the band on her own for three years.

Despite the extraordinary effect of her scat singing in Lady Be Good, you still never get the sense that she raises the effort-level of her singing too high. This is probably the most effort-level you will hear from her, and yet it is still isn't that high — her artistry lay precisely in the fact that she could do something this impressive (and this difficult!) and make it sound as if it were just like a stroll in the park for her.

'THE BEST IS YET TO COME' – PEGGY LEE (1961)

Discovered by Benny Goodman when she was singing in Chicago, Peggy Lee replaced Helen Forrest as Goodman's lead vocalist for two years before moving on. She doesn't credit her years as a Big Band singer as having influenced her style, as much as a discovery she felt she made while singing in a club in Palm Springs very early in her career. As the story goes, she was singing in her usual full, powerful vocal sound while all around her the audience was talking, drinking and generally ignoring the band and its vocalist. She decided to try something different and began singing in a very soft, intimate tone. Suddenly, the audience began to listen. The story may be apocryphal, but the gentle minimalism of her vocal approach is one of her distinctive trademarks. She makes this track (a surprisingly hard melody line to pitch correctly) sound so simple. This is really a composite of her style – that very staccato neutral thick-fold in the mid-range which gives her real power when she wants it, which is often then married to the sweet melt into an Aspirate voice quality – sexy and playful. She loves the microphone and has great intimacy with the listener because of that, which is the benefit for singers of sound technology having come so far by this point. And she's got that bedrock requirement of Jazz singing: absolutely perfect pitching. (In its varied forms, Jazz usually allows so much coming away from the beat and the melody that only singers with extraordinary ears can really keep their place harmonically.) She uses clean diction, very little vibrato and lots of quick compression on endings. There are nice changes in voice quality – from Belt to a whispery upper end with thin-folds. At this point, she typifies the urban 'cool' sound that so many of the Big Band singers came to personify after the Big Band era had passed. She remains cool here, because she largely keeps the effort-level very low – as if teasing with the power and then pulling right back. Even in the middle-8, where she begins to use her bigger Belt sound, she caps each phrase with a very clipped finish and never goes in for the long sustained sound that would have raised her effort-level here. She finishes the song with a very cool, very low effort-level sexy sound that just puts the whole thing together as a sophisticated reading. This is a 'Jazz' track, not because she has dazzling vocal improvisation or uses the voice like an instrument so much, but because she quietly impresses with absolutely solid musicianship and she allows that to be a more important feature than any immediate vocal 'colour'. She doesn't feel that she has to *work* at singing about love. Like other cool, sophisticated city folk, she keeps her cards close to her chest. This is part of that Jazz dichotomy: hot licks on the trumpet, cool licks from the vocalist.

'IN THE WEE SMALL HOURS OF THE MORNING' – FRANK SINATRA (1955)

There are those who would argue that Sinatra is not a Jazz singer; that his style is more accurately described as 'easy listening' or 'middle of the road'; but I think this misses so much about what he achieved as an artist. Sinatra began early with Big Bands, singing first with Harry James and then with Tommy Dorsey. His impressive sense of musicianship and 'swing' influenced everything he did as a singer. This track is vintage Sinatra – his style has now mellowed and matured. And I think this song typifies the way in which Sinatra 'masculinised' popular singing. Against singers like Bing Crosby or Perry Como (whose work always retained a lighter, more 'crooned' sound), or Dick Haymes or Billy Eckstine (who employed a deeper, more resonant but still perceptively 'sung' sound), Sinatra's style seemed seriously male. It is very intimate and, although undoubtedly very satisfying musically and certainly 'sung', it has a perceptively spoken feel about it. In other words, he was singing, but never in a way that made you think first about his voice. Instead, with Sinatra, you always feel as if you've been dropped into a world of dream or heartache or love, and you have to hear *what* he was saying first. On second and third listening you begin to appreciate *how* he was saying it.

Although possessed of an amazing instrument, you can hear that he's adopted a kind of intimacy of style. Like Peggy Lee, he clearly loves the microphone and caresses it in an extraordinary way. He doesn't always exploit the power of his voice; instead here, in the little cracks and flaws of the voice, you hear the battle scars of a man whose love life has been tough – how else to explain the reluctant way in which he releases the sound of the word 'lonely'? He remains almost entirely in a neutral thick-fold sound and he employs very gentle note bends either up or down to ease us into the melody.

People so often talk about Sinatra's phrasing, but generally find it hard to articulate just exactly what they mean by that. I think you can hear it pretty plainly in this track. He innately understands the way in which spoken phrasing is sometimes completely at odds with the often too-even rhythm imposed by musical structure, and he's very smart about not letting that evenness destroy the more natural spoken rhythm of words. A great example of this is the way he manipulates the 'sing-songy-ness' of a phrase like 'never ever' by closing very quickly on the final 'r' sound – we are immediately relieved of the cliché rhymed sound that results from dwelling on the 'eh' vowel sound. He does a similar thing at the end of this phrase with the word 'counting', where he cleverly lingers over the first syllable to prevent the whole of the line from sounding too evenly rhymed and thereby too 'artful' or contrived to contain the full heartbreak he means to convey here. These are small things, notable in one single phrase of the track, but they add up to just what it is that constitutes his brilliance.

He's creaking into some of his onsets and even allows a little scratched or creaked sustain in the voice towards the note finishes. He closes down the vowel sounds of the sustains very quickly so that even when he does sustain a pitch, it never sounds 'sung' in the way it would if he remained open on an 'ooh' or 'aah' vowel sound. He often moves very smoothly from consonant to consonant with just a slight and vulnerable, fluttery vibrato to ease the transition. The great thing about his style is the way in which his extra-ordinary musicality, which makes everything move so smoothly, is at odds with the intimate and conversational sound that he achieves by closing his vowels so quickly and allowing those creaked and scratched sounds into a very clean diction.

The diction isn't overworked – it's just a bonus of finishing with the held consonant so often. And he has a natural sense of how to finish even tough consonant sounds without overemphasising them (listen to the way he gently insinuates the 'k' sound at the end of 'awake' in the first verse). As the track proceeds he grows more clever with the placement of the phrase, almost never coming down on the beat but shifting just slightly ahead or behind the beat to allow a conversational rather than a sung rhythm to dominate the feel of performance. And that was both the absolute wonder and the great secret of Sinatra's style at the height of his powers: he was singing to millions but it always feels as if he's talking to *you*.

'ALMOST BLUE' – DIANA KRALL (2004)

This is a contemporary cover of Chet Baker's classic and his influence seems to remain very strongly in this track. In keeping with Jazz style, the effort-level here is really low. Even though Krall often begins a phrase with a hard glottal or consonant sound and comes in with neutral thick-fold, she usually quickly pulls back into a thin-fold then Aspirate sound and quick com-pressed, sometimes aspirated, often creaked finishes that add up to a very intimate sound. You get the sense that without a very good and sensitive mic you wouldn't hear much of this performance live. She employs some unusual note bends, both up and down, which gives a very loose and languid feel to the piece. Her voice floats in a silky way over and around the small combo accompaniment; usually well behind the beat in her phrasing. She particularly favours lengthening the sounds of words mid-phrase, which gives the track an interesting kind of 'stretched out' sound. She builds the song very subtly, rarely ever coming into full voice – particularly where most vocalists would go for the big sound, she draws back and adds just that bit more air or Creak into the mix of the sound. She's isn't flashy with improvisation, and is perfectly happy to simply ease a phrase in or out with a few small additional notes or 'twiddles'; at no point here does she ever really move or drive the song along in the way that some great Jazz singers do. But she's dead accurate in her pitching and overall the sound is incredibly sophisticated and intelligent. That, combined with things like a rather unexpected long, slow Aspirate fall, make the whole piece add up to a beautiful modern take on the gentle Jazz vocal sound of singers like Baker or Billie Holiday.

SUMMARY

Jazz is a very broad church and at its most intimidating it includes vocalists with nearly superhuman powers of spontaneous musicality and accuracy (Ella Fitzgerald, Bobby McFerrin, Al Jarreau). But in its more common form, Jazz is the medium in which artists, both instrumental and vocal, really work to achieve a kind of equality. The 'lead' sounds are usually equally divided between the singers and the players, and that requires a sort of common language in the overall approach to a song. The most common vocal qualities that define a Jazz performance are:

1. Predominantly low effort or low perceived effort-level in performance, which often means lighter vocal qualities and/or less sustain.
2. Generally very few (and sometimes no) changes of vocal quality within a song.
3. Quick, often compressed or falling finishes.
4. Great accuracy of pitching.
5. Enough improvisational ability to allow the singer to adapt a song to fit within the musical world in which it is being performed.
6. A strong rhythmic sense that allows the fundamental 'swing' or syncopation of the music to come alive.
7. An easy sense of play and freedom in the delivery.

PRACTICE

1. Jazz is playful, and play takes courage. You need to really listen to Jazz artists before you can find the courage, I think, to see just how far you can push things. It's helpful to listen to Jazz instrumentalists as well as Jazz vocalists, and I've listed some suggestions in the Resources section.

2. Once you've spent some time really listening, put on the demo CD, and chose either track 23 (for a very 'straight' accompaniment) or or track 25 (for a slightly more jazzy feel) and listen to the accompaniment a few times. (The key may not be perfect, but C seems to fit general male/female ranges. Jazz style is extremely forgiving in terms of vocal quality, so don't worry if you're working a little higher or lower than usual – that could be helpful in terms of keeping your effort-level low.)

3. Now try singing through a few times, but don't allow yourself to start a phrase right on the beat – come in either before or after the beat:

Swing low sweet chariot
Comin for to carry me home
Swing low sweet chariot
Comin for to carry me home.
If you get to heaven before I do
Comin for to carry me home
Tell all my friends I'm comin there too
Comin for to carry me home

4. Sing through again, with your concentration in various areas. First, try staying in predominantly one voice quality and keep sustains to an absolute minimum. Try again, and this time compress or Aspirate or fall off the notes as often as you can. Feel free to experiment with onsets, but keep them low effort-level. Keep working through your 'boredom threshold' with these exercises – you need to be so comfortable with the song that you can be really playful with it.

5. Finally, try singing *anything* except the melody. It might help you to get someone else to sing the melody quietly with you, while you look for other possibilities. If you do this exercise, just tell yourself that you must try not to sing whatever the other person is singing. You don't need to do any great extended improv on this – just gentle variations away from the melody will help you greatly to understand what all your possibilities are for extending and playing when you go back to singing the melody.

You might find that you do better working all of the exercises above with a (karaoke?) backing track for a song that you really like. Making an emotional connection with a song always gives your playfulness a little charge. If any of this came easily to you, you're probably a Jazz 'natural'. If not – keep listening, and keep experimenting. If this style is really foreign to you, make the effort to spend much more time listening. It will pay off in every other style you *do* feel comfortable in, because listening and working with Jazz style can really increase your sense of melodic and rhythmic confidence.

Country

In 1949, the editors at Billboard, then as now the American music industry's most important trade magazine, announced a change in the nomenclature they would use to label different genres. Henceforth, what had previously been classified as . . .'folk' music would be called 'Country and Western'.[8]

At the same time that 'race' records were reclassified as 'Rhythm & Blues', records that had been selling as 'Folk' were also rebranded. From a contemporary perspective it may seem a bit strange, since we probably wouldn't see these two genres as particularly similar now. In this section I'll be looking at Country as a genre and not including Western – which was a pretty distinct style of its own, and actually much more of a 'pop' genre. Western really grew in combination with transplanted dust bowl farmers from Texas and Oklahoma who found themselves in California around the same time that early cowboy films were coming out of Hollywood. Singing cowboys like

8 Miller, *Almost Grown*, p.44

Gene Autry and Roy Rogers were Hollywood stars, and certainly never lived as cowboys. In a sense it was a kind of 'made-up' style – some of it (especially in its 'Southwest Shuffle' incarnation) quite wonderful. But Country in its early phase was a much more organic thing. Like early Blues singers, seminal Country artists like Jimmie Rodgers, Hank Williams and Loretta Lynn genuinely lived the lives they sang about. They had a number of similarities with Blues artists despite the wide differences in style. Country music dwells on the same kind of subject matter that Blues does but in a generally much less defiant way. Where Blues singers often found ways to bring humour and a kind of determination to survive the worst in both their lyrics and their performances, the Country artists often wholeheartedly give way to their despair. Particularly in the ballad form, Country songs can be a sustained exercise in really allowing that despair to work itself through musically.

In many ways, early Country music was the white version of the Blues. It evolved from its early Folk roots through influences from early Jazz and Blues styles, but nevertheless remained for some time stubbornly *un*refined as a genre and pitched its appeal to a poor rural (Southern) white working-class audience. Like the Blues, Country based its appeal in authentic experience, in hardship, in living off the land, in survival; but somehow Country always did so in a more theatrical sense. Its themes were similar to those found in Blues music and centred around the everyday tragedies of love, loss and hard work; or on the common consolations of love, sex and drinking – but it did so much more, I would argue, through a sense of the singer as almost theatrical (or melodramatic) character.

As with early Blues, most of early Country was acoustic guitar-based and composed of simple chord patterns. But its overriding distinction – and the distinction that it was socially forced to maintain – was that Country was a white musical form. This meant that against the rise of popular music and the widespread availability of radio music shows in the early decades of this century, Country artists were facing (whether consciously or not) a unique difficulty: how to create an identifiably white musical style/sound through a body of music that had so many similarities to what was an already well-established body of black musical sounds. Of course, in this situation radio only forced the issue: if the listener couldn't *see* whether the singer was white or black, then the listener had to try to discern the colour difference simply through the sound of the singer's voice. And despite the many similarities in background and musical form, when one listens now to early Blues and to early Country singers, their stylistic differences are marked.

At the most basic level, you can hear an accent in the singing that pretty neatly identifies the genre. Country singers nearly always employ a detectable southern drawl, and that drawl itself has a kind of Twang in the tone of it and a 'bend' in the melody of it – both of which heavily influence style in Country singing. Despite the many fusion forms of contemporary Country singing, there are some clear traits that run straight through from Jimmie Rodgers and Hank Williams to Kenny Chesney, or from Patsy Cline and Tammy Wynette through to Deana Carter.

On the whole I don't often encounter students who want to work on this style – Pop, Rock, Gospel and Jazz being generally the areas that most want to explore. But the style has been so influential in Rock music, and has produced artists of such distinction, that I always include it when I'm teaching vocal style and students have always found pleasure (if unexpectedly!) in experimenting with it.

'YOUR CHEATIN' HEART' AND 'HEY, GOOD LOOKIN'' – HANK WILLIAMS (1951)

Hank Williams was perhaps the greatest of the early Country 'icons', and I think that much of what distinguishes Country sound is clearly evident in his voice in these two seminal tracks. A raw, nasal Twang, and a direct, unfussy delivery typified his style. In *Your Cheatin' Heart*, his heavy reliance on the Flip onset pushes the ear right up into the sound – creating the opposite effect of the downward inflection of Blues delivery. You can hear the influence of early Country 'yodelers' like Rodgers in the Williams sound, and he uses that yodel extensively in tracks like *Lovesick Blues*. The tone is 'unschooled', and almost painfully raw sometimes, but still has a 'sung' sound – in other words, it's musical and exploits the sustain of sound. This creates a very different sound from the 'spoken' delivery and Rumble of so many Blues artists. Sustains are longer, and while vibrato is rare, Williams tends to finish his long phrases with a heavily bent note attack (you can hear this particularly on the word 'me' in *Hey Good Lookin'*), and a lengthy sustain with no vibrato, that finishes in a little fall off the note. Longer sustains mid-phrase contribute to the more 'sung' feeling of his songs, yet the unrefined tone still manages to create what so many of the Blues singers did: the sense that the listener is hearing a kind of primal emotional sound from an artist who has lived though much and who values that experience over any kind of fancy 'artistry'.

In *Hey, Good Lookin'*, Williams' bright, Twangy sound seems to capture wonderfully the optimism and good-time feel of his lyric, which sets the scene with great detail: the hot rod ford and the two-dollar bill that Williams uses to entice the unknown woman were the dreams of a common man and his vocal performance is common in the very best sense – there is absolutely nothing sophisticated or premeditated about it. He does nothing to beautify the 'hillbilly' identifiers of his nasal, drawling sound, and the effect is almost like looking through a camera lens at a scene that most of us have never seen anywhere except perhaps on film. But in Williams' time, no doubt, the match of sound to experience would have had real resonance with his audience, and that audience would have responded to the raw honesty of his work.

There are many 'flaws' detectable in this track – his sustains employ a certain 'generosity' of pitch, and sometimes he works them hard enough to push a bit of scratchiness in the sound. His tone releases are almost entirely rather wayward falls from the note – not elegant in any sense. On the whole, he employs less 'flip' in his sound here (either in onset or in glide between notes) than he does, for example, in *Your Cheatin' Heart*, where the Flip and a more gentle, darker sustain with mild vibrato brings a bit of relief to the long, pretty relentless nasal Twang sustains of this song. Despite these flaws and the admission that at its most hard and focused point, Williams' Twang is probably the opposite of vocal beauty, I still respond at once to what I find irresistibly life-affirming and exuberant in the performance.

Perhaps more than that, in this track I see a perfect match of form and content. Somehow, *Hey, Good Lookin'*, as a song, makes life seem inviting. The pleasures Williams sings about are both easy and immediate. Lyrics about free soda pop and dancing might seem absurdly innocent to a contemporary audience, but Williams creates a compelling sort of philosophy from these simple things. And combined with the raw sincerity of Hank's performance, the whole song seems to make life sound uncomplicated, with pleasure accessible to anyone.

Despite some similarities in both Blues and Country styles, there seems no doubt that Hank Williams' voice is the voice of a white man. It has the thin nasality of certain white Southern dialects and I am willing to bet that no one in the Southern states at the time of Williams' recordings would have come to any other conclusion. Country audiences were not looking for anything other than 'ordinary' folks singing of 'ordinary' life and experiences, so that to some extent early Country artists, from Minnie Pearl to Ernest Tubbs, seemed to feel obligated to present a non-glamorous image to accompany this non-glamorised vocal style.

The general suspicion of these audiences was that anything too sophisticated was bound to be dishonest in some way, but this notion was never without its tensions – from 'rhinestone cowboys' to 'big hair', Country music has tended to fashion its own version of acceptable glamour. Unlike the change that one could trace in the Blues-to-Jazz crossover artists like Billie Holiday or Ethel Waters (where increasingly sophisticated audiences demanded increasingly sophisticated music), Country musicians perhaps found themselves drawn to slicker presentations in sequins and heavy emotion, but the musical simplicity and 'authenticity' (however melodramatically manu-factured!) of the Country sound remains a touchstone of this style.

'D.I.V.O.R.C.E.' – TAMMY WYNETTE (1968)

Tammy Wynette's *D.I.V.O.R.C.E.* is a much later track than Hank Williams' *Hey, Good Lookin'*. As such, although it employs stylistic elements found in early Country, it was produced at the point where I believe Country songs had pretty commonly moved from the raw emotional dramas of Hank Williams' *I'm So Lonesome I Could Cry* or Patsy Cline's *Crazy*, into full-blown melodrama. Like so many Country songs (*Did I Shave My Legs for This?*, *Thank God and Greyhound You're Gone*, *Get Your Tongue Out of my Mouth, I'm Kissing You Goodbye*), a comic title belies a soap-opera content and delivery. *D.I.V.O.R.C.E.* is a good example of the aforementioned tendency towards theatricality, and the overplayed sentimentality of Tammy Wynette's vocal choices here move an already pretty soppy song into the territory of kitsch. Indeed, the song is considered by many to be a camp classic.

I think it's important to stress that I don't necessarily think this is a bad thing. Melodrama/campness may or may not be to your taste, but most vocal-ists know that there are times when a bit of carefully judged vocal 'over-egging' can have a real impact. And *D.I.V.O.R.C.E.* is quite a pudding. The lyrics are, in themselves, so contrived that it's doubtful anyone would want to try this song with a middle-ground sort of delivery. It's an all-or-nothing proposition, and Wynette's voice is perfectly placed to make the whole commitment.

Because it is pure storytelling, Wynette is careful about diction. Generally, Country singers are careful about diction because so many of the songs are reliant on the listener's ability to understand the tale they tell. From great songs like Marty Robbins' *El Paso* to Kenny Rogers' *The Gambler*, this is a genre that has always rewarded a good yarn. *D.I.V.O.R.C.E.* is an old-fashioned tear-jerker that employees some pretty straightforward emotional techniques. Wynette's overall aim is to invite the listener to share/believe in her pain. It's a somewhat strange experience, though, since she makes only a few vocal choices and sticks rather rigidly to them. This removes the sense of spontaneity from the performance (a spontaneity that Blues and Gospel trade heavily in) and perhaps this is what gives the performance a rather theatrical feel.

Throughout the song her delivery has regularity. Phrases are weighted quite evenly and for the most part placement is like clockwork. Occasionally you can hear a slight backphrasing at work in the verse, but it's rare and the chorus phrases are always delivered right on the beat. As the song progresses the 'D.I.V.O.R.C.E.' lyric works in a rather bizarre counter time against the backing track which reinforces the 'right-on-the-beat' feel of the performance. The overriding vocal choice of the track is a fairly quick Flip onset and short but definite upward bends in the note attack. Combined with a vulnerable-sounding thin-fold tone (which is the only vocal quality detectable in the piece) and a series of quick, compressed releases, this makes the whole performance sound like the imitation of a crying woman. The important word here, I suppose, is 'imitation', because at no point (at least in a close listening) does it feel as if the crying could be real – the whole track feels too closely regulated for that; but the combination of an artful impression of crying and the sentimentality of lyric seemed to prove a very potent combination for Country fans, as this was a huge hit for Tammy Wynette and remains a 'classic' of the genre. That little 'cry' or 'catch' in the voice has remained an important part of Country style – it lends an immediate (if, again, theatrical) sense of heartbreak to the listener.

The effort-level is relatively low – both perceived and true. This is another factor which prevents us from experiencing the song as something raw or direct – and in that sense Wynette differs here from many Country artists, who tend to prefer the exact middle-ground when it comes to effort-level – neither low nor extremely high. This middle-ground effort-level is a pretty consistent trait of Country, and one that strongly distinguishes it from Blues and Gospel. Nearly every complementary element of style can be used by the Country singer to create an emotional effect, but that emotion doesn't seem to spring from raw unmediated energy. *Hey, Good Lookin'* is a relatively high effort for a Country song, yet compared to most Gospel or Blues numbers, it's a pretty low-key affair.

There would be any number of ways to read the effects of the low or middling-effort coupled with high-emotion in Country classics, like Kenny Rogers' *Ruby Don't Take Your Love To Town*, or Dolly Parton's version of *I Will Always Love You* (where the effort-level itself does much to distinguish her version from Whitney Houston's soaring, massive effort on the same song), but for me they generally add up to a kind of unabashed vulnerability. Unlike the kind of pain or vulnerability of the Blues singer, Country singers don't always convince me that they're going to make it through this latest crisis. In this context, pain and suffering can become epic – even noble. Of course, not all Country songs *are* about suffering, but the upbeat Country sound often has far fewer distinguishing stylistic elements than the tear-soaked Country ballad – which is why, I think, so many of the most memorable Country songs are the ballads.

We're at the point, of course, where response to stylistic choices remains pretty stubbornly subjective. Your response to these songs may be completely different, or perhaps, like me, Country music wouldn't ordinarily be your first choice when listening to music. But there is much to learn from the boldness of such artists and the greatest challenge for any vocalist is to make their choices well – the more you have to choose from, the greater the possibilities.

SUMMARY

Country music in its early phase was not a 'crossover' genre. The rare crossover hits were the exception that proved the rule. These days, of course, it can sometimes be quite a challenge to distinguish Country singers from Pop singers, since there has been such a great fusion within the sound. But overall, the strong stylistic tendencies of its early days remain influential in County music still, and if you're interested in exploring this style, find a song that you feel real affinity for (preferably one with a good story!) and then work through it, observing the following common Country singing characteristics:

1. A strong reliance on heavier vocal qualities (Belt, Twang, neutral thick-fold), although generally employed in a middle-range rather than a high effort-level (which, if used, would probably result in a Rock sound).
2. A tendency towards very even phrase weighting and placement – syncopation or improvisation is rare in this style.
3. There tends to be very little variation of vocal quality in Country, so keep your vocal quality pretty consistent. The majority of songs are sung in neutral thick-fold with a middling effort, and although Belt is used, it is rarely a high-effort-level Belt.
4. Most Country songs have a very strong, 'sung' sound – long sustains are common, as is vibrato, although it is often combined with a compressed finish rather than a fade (which would make the sound more refined and less gutsy). Country singers don't attempt to 'sweeten' the sound.

5. There isn't a lot of play in dynamics or sung volume levels – songs don't tend to 'build' to a high point or go from a scream to a whisper. It's a very consistent style in terms of both tone and effort all the way through a song.
6. There is limited use of the different elements of style. Onsets tend to be the most varied part of the Country sound, but even here there is not a wide variation. Stick to fairly hard Glottals, and Simultaneous onsets (coming in right on the beat of course!) and Flip or Creak, which are fairly common.
7. Even contemporary Country singers still tend to sing with a heavy Southern American accent, which gives a natural upward bend in the note attack and a rather Twangy sound, even when in neutral thick-fold.
8. Songs tend to be delivered with a kind of melodramatic intensity, so you need to make sure that you've chosen a song with lyrics that you can put real feeling behind.

Rock

It could be said that in many ways, Rock'n'Roll began when the hard distinctions between black and white music began to dissolve. That doesn't mean the segregated market didn't continue, as it does now, but it does mean that the early Rock artists were happy to blend Blues, Country and Hillbilly styles together to form a high-energy fusion sound (often referred to early on as 'Jump Blues') that revolutionised the music industry. Of all the styles we've looked at so far, Rock is the most difficult to categorise because it *is* such a fusion. It's also probably the most impossible to prescribe practice for (I won't even try!) because historically, it isn't so much a form as an energy. It takes the rawness of Blues, the playfulness of Jazz, the melodrama of Country and extreme high energy of Gospel and then sort of explodes over a highly amplified musical backing. What made it so distinct, despite the fact that it is a genuinely derivative form, is most apparent in the very early works, so I'll keep my analysis centred on a few of the classics and one contemporary homage to a classic Rock sound.

'DON'T BE CRUEL' AND 'HEARTBREAK HOTEL' – ELVIS PRESLEY (1956)

Situated at the perfect junction between Blues, Hillbilly and Country music, the overall energy and drive of Elvis' music lifted it stylistically away from anything that had gone on prior to his first recordings and appearances. Because he was white and because he was working with a guitar/bass musical accompaniment, Presley was initially marketed as a Country singer. One of his very first appearances was on the Grand Ole Opry, where he sang *Blue Moon of Kentucky*. But like so many white Southerner artists of his time, he'd spent much time listening to and being influenced by black Blues artists:

> I'd play along with the radio or phonograph. We were a religious family going around to sing together at camp meetings and revivals, and I'd take my guitar with us when I could. I also dug the real low-down Mississippi singers, mostly Big Bill Broonzy and [Arthur] Big Boy Crudup, although they would scold me at home for listening to them.[9]

He had even attended a local Black Baptist church where he was no doubt influenced by Gospel music. Given these influences, he represented a challenge for DJs and marketing people alike. At the first sign of success with *That's All Right*, Sam Phillips (legendary owner of Sun Records, where Elvis recorded his first works) recalled the problems of having found such a unique artist, when one disc jockey told him that Presley 'was so Country he shouldn't be played after 5 a.m.' while the Country DJs 'said he was too black for them'.[10] Phillips quickly arranged a radio interview with his young singer, and the DJ asking the questions made sure that he worked in a question that would allow Elvis to state that he had attended the 'whites-only' Humes High School, just so that the listeners would be in no doubt about his racial identity.

But his voice was particularly flexible and unique, and when you go back to listen to some of his early classics, it's clear why he was such a compelling mystery. Although white artists covering songs by black artists was nothing new at the point at which Elvis was doing it, the difficulty in classifying his sound, and the extraordinary playfulness in his vocal approach (along with the bizarre nervous tics of his early stage performances, which he learned to exaggerate in order to induce squeals from delighted audiences) made him stand out as a pioneer of a new kind of music. In a piece like *Don't Be Cruel* you can hear that he's fearlessly exploring – and there's so much going on. His confidence has grown in the years between the early Sun recordings and

9 Elvis Presley, quoted in Peter Guralnick, *Feel Like Going Home* (Edinburgh: Canongate Publishers, 2003), p. 172/3
10 Guralnick, *Feel Like Going Home*, p. 173

these two tracks, and he's really come into what is so unique and exciting in his sound. There's a definite percussive edge to the note delivery and attack. His diction ranges wildly from clean and crisp to a strange sort of contrived slur. He employs a whole range of onsets here from hard Glottal to Flip to Aspirate. His finishes are extreme compressions, which gives the track a wonderful percussive, rather than 'sung', sound in the delivery. There's no flow at all to the line – he leaves that to the Jordanaires, who 'bop-bop' or croon away in the background. This highly clipped delivery feels very much as if it all happens in the throat; he's glottal-stopping all the way to keep that extreme compression jumpy and alive, and sometimes adds a quick 'catch in the throat' that sounds rather like a very compressed Flip. His improvs are strange affairs – mostly a few oddly negotiated sliding up and down sounds at the beginning of phrases. He uses audible breath and a few Aspirate finishes to give this a slight sense of high effort, although the true effort-level is rather middling. He stays in neutral thick-fold or speech with only occasional jumps up into a single note in thin-fold, or the occasional exaggerated Elongated quality in places like the repeat 'thinking of' lyric. He uses a bit of fluttery vibrato just occasionally, which lends a little vulnerability to an otherwise very upbeat, edgy delivery, and his phrase weight is very even here as he works against the tightly rhythmic backing in the verses.

Heartbreak Hotel is still more extraordinary in the range of stylistic elements he employs. Although it is a ballad, he's so bold in his exploration that it stands well away from the straighter and duller ballad sounds he settled down with once his career was more advanced. There is more sustain and vibrato here, as you would expect with a ballad, but the vibrato is fast and fluttery which lends a sense of pain and vulnerability to sound. The sheer number of vocal quality changes and stylistic flourishes lend the song a high perceived effort-level. He throws the energy heavily at the top of each verse and then lets the clean diction and attack 'melt' into an Elongated quality towards the finish of the verse (on the 'so lonely') to suggest a kind of emotional break-down. He was a master of using the Elongated quality to great effect, and he combines it here with Creak, Aspirate quality and percussion to give it real power. That sound itself is then further subverted by the playful and percussive sounds in the chorus; these recall the defiance of the best of Blues ebullience.

Because there is such a lot of stylistic exploration and vocal quality change going on, the dynamics of the song vary wildly from the high-energy Twang of the verse openings to the mumbled play of the choruses. His approach is highly theatrical, but convincing for all that. Because of the spontaneous feel of the piece and the outrageous vocal choices he's making, this song never descends into camp but instead feels honest and raw – just right for a Rock ballad. He could not have lent these recordings such style had he not had great energy and courage in exploring. That energy and courage, along with a kind of defiance in the face of what might constitute 'legitimate' singing, is what gives Rock vocal its definition.

'TUTTI FRUTTI' – LITTLE RICHARD (1956)

The story of this recording is legend. Little Richard, whose stage persona was incredibly flamboyant and energetic, found himself completely unable to bring those qualities into the recording studio, where he was working on a dull slow ballad called *Lonesome and Blue*. Disillusioned, both producer and artist took a break and during lunch at a local club, Little Richard jumped up on the bandstand and began singing one of his more outrageous live concert songs. The original lyrics were far too racy to record, so they were rewritten in an afternoon by a local songwriter and they went back into the studio to record *Tutti Frutti*. The track sums up so much of why he was and remains an extraordinary influence in the Rock vocal sound. He was heavily influenced by artists like Louis Jordan and Ruth Brown, particularly in terms of energy and that massively pushed release sound that occurs so often in tracks like *Tutti Frutti*.

Perhaps the greatest distinction of his sound is the energy. No matter what he's doing, the perceived effort-level is always incredibly high. Little Richard does absolutely nothing that a voice teacher would approve of. There's no trace of 'good' singing here: it's pure raw energy and joy. In the early verses, he's simple – he keeps the sustains short and uses mostly a constricted voice quality to achieve the sound of raw energy. This kind of rumbled sound, while similar to Louis Armstrong's, was not the nearly permanent quality of the voice that it was for Armstrong. With Richard, it was clear that this constricted sound was a choice and if you listen to other tracks recorded in the same year (e.g. *Slippin and Slidin'*) you can hear that when he chooses to sing without it, he has a warm sandy tone similar to Sam Cooke's. He weights both the opening and the finishes of his phrases, although not consistently: often he simply doesn't bother to complete some phrases, and he employs almost no sustain. He compresses finishes without falling off a note and indeed will often push a note ending up with great energy and volume. Where a Gospel release frequently ends with a hard exhalation of air, Little Richard pushes that exhalation into a high short scream. It's an extraordinary sound which seems to suggest that nothing can really contain his energy as it spills out far beyond the end of the phrase. His improvs tend to be through a highly energised 'whooo' falsetto sound – a sound that many subsequent Rock singers employed. He didn't bring much more than raw unmediated energy to market, but that alone made him highly distinct from the 'Pop' male vocalists of the day like Pat Boone (whose bland cover version of *Tutti Frutti* is considered below). His refusal to follow the rules in singing style influenced a great many artists to come; from James Brown and Otis Redding to Paul McCartney (see Section Five), whose work in many places emulated Little Richard's kind of 'primal scream' sound.

'RUN DEVIL RUN' – PAUL MCCARTNEY (1999)

This is really classic McCartney Rock sound and demonstrates why he's such an exciting singer when he lets loose in this style. It's a 'straight' performance from him. Compared with other pieces on the CD, this is his most raw, unmediated approach, and there's very little manipulation of the sound he's making. It gives this track an extraordinary directness and, in contrast to his performances on *Movie Magg* or *Brown Eyed Handsome Man*, feels as if it comes straight from the heart – artless and pure. It probably helps that he wrote the piece, since he's an artist who is much more at home with his own material than when covering material by other writers.

The phrase placement is pretty even (the track feels really packed, so he has little choice but to keep the placement even), although there's just the slight back phrase throughout. He uses quick compressed releases in all cases, with a falling inflection at the ends of verses. The phrases are so choppy and unsustained that he could almost be speaking to you – but the energy-level is extremely high and he's Belting throughout. This is almost a Rock 'patter' song – very wordy, in the style of old Chuck Berry tunes. The opening phrases feature some bend in the note attack but most of the rest of the verse work is very straight in terms of note attack, and this takes away nearly all sense of the performance being 'sung'. He is clever about introducing just the hint of Constriction throughout the song, though he doesn't really come into any full-blown constricted sounds until the very end, where his final note on 'run' cracks with the weight of such driving energy behind it. He loves that classic high thin-fold 'oooh' sound that made so many appearances in his Beatles days and here, in the middle-8 section, it provides the only real vocal quality change in the entire piece. By his own admission this piece is a homage to Chuck Berry and it actually takes the Berry style up quite a few notches in terms of energy. This is pure pastiche – it's a British take on southern American culture of at least half a century ago, but somehow the whole thing adds up in a very satisfying way. The performance is wholly aimed at appealing to us on a visceral level and towards setting a kind of wild and reckless mood, which is more or less what Rock always sets out to do. This piece, like so many of Chuck Berry's, actually features quite a well-crafted lyric/story, but the story is subservient to the overall energy and sonic experience that's meant to get into our blood and get us up and moving. To that end, he's not singing a story for us so much as he's trying to urge us to forget our inhibitions and dance all night. I have no doubt that in a live setting it would achieve just that.

SUMMARY
Rock, like Blues, is a style that doesn't reward a 'sung' sound. It needs a more immediate, straight-from-the-heart kind of sound that may come in a whisper or may come in a scream, but however it is delivered we want to be absolutely certain that the singer is holding nothing back. Because of this, we're not primarily concerned with the beauty of tone – although a great number of good Rock singers like Freddie Mercury, Billy Joel or Bono happen to have great tone as well as passion.

Rock singers rarely work without a heavily amplified and percussive accompaniment, so it can be quite difficult to attempt practice in this style without a band working alongside you. Often singers are asked to bring Rock song into Musical Theatre auditions, and this can be quite tricky – not least because you will be expected to work with only piano accompaniment and often that pianist will not know your song or will have very little sense of Rock 'feel' in the playing. That means I usually advise students to bring in songs that are associated with Rock artists, and to do their best to work through the most common elements of Rock style, which are:

1. Predominantly thick-fold vocal qualities: either neutral thick-fold, Belt or Twang. Changes from one vocal quality to another tend to be abrupt rather than 'artfully' negotiated.
2. Voice quality changes are often kept to a minimum.
3. Consistently high effort-level in the performance, both true and perceived.
4. Sustains or fades of any kind are relatively uncommon – most finishes are compressed, falling or variations on Gospel releases.

5. A wide variety of onsets is employed, although the high-effort onsets – Flip, Glottal, Constricted or Rumbled onsets are most common.
6. A fearless exploration of sound in performance, which frequently means the use of some constricted or 'dangerous' qualities that – by sheer effort – convince us of the singer's raw passion and energy.

This last element is, of course, negotiable by the singer. As we've noted, many voices can sustain very little use of these dangerous qualities. In a Musical Theatre audition setting, that doesn't matter much – it would be quite hard to employ the massive effort-levels required by Rock when the singer is accompanied by full band rather than just piano. But the first five common elements of this style will certainly see you through if you couple them with a great passion for whatever song you're singing. That will be really important when you're trying to find the abandon needed for this style.

Pop

Because we've looked at some very early examples of style in popular music, it seems logical to conclude with a look at contemporary Pop, which is a fusion of all these styles. But if it is difficult to define Jazz or Blues or Country, it is that much more difficult to define Pop. Of course, on the simplest level, Pop is popular music – or whatever has mass appeal – and you could certainly argue that forms of Jazz, Country, Rock and Blues have had extraordinary mass appeal over much of the last century; you might therefore conclude that they are Pop music. But that tends *not* to be what we commonly think of as 'Pop' music these days. The rapid rise of the record industry after the Second World War, which fuelled an enormous amount of activity in songwriting and recording, coupled with the equally rapid growth in radio and television output, meant that from the 1950s onwards, styles in music (and therefore in singing) have blurred to the point where it gets increasingly difficult to talk confidently about what 'style' a singer is working in. Nevertheless, it seems pretty easy for most people to conclude that singers like Madonna, Kylie Minogue, Will Young and Britney Spears are 'Pop' singers. ABBA is a 'Pop' band, and when people audition for the musical *Mamma Mia!* they are told to bring 'Pop' songs instead of Musical Theatre songs.

There is a kind of tendency to think of Pop singers as bland and a bit disposable – *great* voices are rarely thought of as Pop voices. There's nothing wrong at all with Madonna's voice or Kylie's voice – but you wouldn't mistake them for Tina Turner or Chaka Kahn. In fact, great voices don't make particularly good Pop singers, as Barbra Streisand pretty neatly proved in her few unsuccessful forays into Pop music. That might be because good Pop music is usually much more about the song than it is about the singer. This is also why so many Pop singers come and go relatively quickly. The rare few who do remain around (*like* Madonna, Kylie or Robbie Williams) have to work extremely hard to bring the focus onto themselves as performing personalities.

This is, of course, the great irony of shows like *Pop Idol*. Most 'idols' in music have *not* been Pop singers – Elvis Presley was many things, but he was not a Pop singer. Paul McCartney, Mick Jagger, Bruce Springsteen or Bono all took their influences from a variety of sources, but in the end you wouldn't call any of them Pop singers.

Great Pop songs, however, tend to have real staying power. The whole purpose of the Pop song is to be memorable – not generally for great or profound lyrics or complex, compelling harmonic structure (although some do achieve this), but in much simpler terms – their repetitive structure and accessible tunes get stuck in your head. The best Pop songs written by Stock, Aitken and Waterman would not be well served by a great singer, since an outstanding voice would obstruct the song's ability to get right inside your head. Consequently, this simple melody/lyric line and Kylie Minogue's light, easy voice singing about being so lucky, lucky, lucky is just the right combination. In an earlier era of Pop singing, Burt Bacharach and Hal David found a similar muse in Dionne Warwick, whose easy musicality combined with a low perceived effort-level proved just right for getting a Pop song like *Do You Know the Way to San José* or *I'll Never Fall in Love Again* 'hooked' into our memories.

Pop draws on all styles and presents them in a 'lite' version. Kylie is somewhere between Rock and Country 'lite'; the Spice Girls were a 'lite' version of Rhythm & Blues. This is only possible when singing voice and material are in themselves pretty lightweight. That doesn't mean unskilled – whatever else one might think of Stock, Aitken and Waterman they are highly skilled Pop writers. You can feel that their songs are carefully crafted, and there is skill in Kylie Minogue's singing. We are concerned with 'craft' when it comes to Pop, and it is not a category that rewards raw honesty or lack of 'art'.

But when both song and voice are remarkable, we're usually out of the Pop category, no matter how much mass appeal a recording may have. Perhaps considering the career of a group like the Beach Boys makes this point. In their early 'Surf'n'Hotrod' recordings, the sound of their traditional close harmonies and easy, swooping melodies made great Pop music – it had an emotional appeal which was charming and shallow, and the easy vocal sound allowed us to focus on the catchy fantasy tunes about being a teenager in Southern California. But as the writing and the lyrics grew more profound, and the voices and the productions grew more complex and sophisticated, they became almost unclassifiable. Songs like *Surf's Up* challenged all the work that they'd done in their first decade and came, for many, to signify a loss of the innocence that had infused their early Pop sound.

Pop music has a long history, of course, so even our responses to it have to be seen in historical contexts. I am aware that a lot of my students currently see Pop music as a genre that appeals to the 'pre-teen' or young teenaged market. I customarily work with students who are 18 years or older, and many of them pretty actively dislike the whole commercial Pop genre and want to find ways to distinguish their sound from it. But whatever you think of Pop in its most commercial form, from my point of view it is probably the hardest style of all to teach.

I think there are a number of reasons for this, but pretty high on the list would be the amount of skill and ease a singer has to possess to do it successfully. Rather like Jazz, Pop has a kind of 'swing' – it isn't the highly sophisticated rhythmic thing that swing can sometimes be in Jazz, but it certainly requires that a singer know how to move around a ground beat comfortably; to improvise with ease (even though not necessarily with great extension); to have extremely good pitch; to be able to shape a phrase so that it has a certain flexibility and sinuousness to it; to understand melodic line but not to get caught up in singing it too 'straight'; to understand the fundamentals of producing a good tone (in that traditional aesthetic sense) but not to sound schooled; to have an easy command of a number of elements of style; and to be able to employ most of them pretty effortlessly. In other words, it's extremely demanding, but must be perceived as quite effortless. And while there are many things about this that can be taught, some are quite difficult.

Even trying to articulate what I mean when I say above that the shape of a phrase needs to have 'a certain sinuousness to it' makes me aware of the paucity of language in trying to describe musical effect at times. But most people who have ever tried to sing/learn/teach Pop music from sheet music will know exactly what I mean. Sometimes that flexibility or sinuousness comes from the build of a Creak or Aspirate onset into a full vocal quality with a light bend that glides effortless into the next note and melts into an Aspirate finish that falls with a light downward bend – Pop style often has a lot of dynamic variation within a phrase. Sometimes it's about the way in which small melodic additions or grace notes are negotiated with some mild swing that makes the singer's glide between the notes feel just that slight bit uneven and gives the little melodic lift some elegance. Sometime it's about negotiating voice-quality changes with craft and ease, and at other times it's about making those 'gear changes' abruptly, as part of the overall effort picture. All this can make it very difficult to help the young singer who has been practising in choral music or on Musical Theatre numbers with a voice teacher all their lives suddenly understand how to make a song like Madonna's *Like a Virgin* really come alive vocally.

Perhaps as we look at a few examples I can make some of this clearer:

'TUTTI FRUTTI'- PAT BOONE (1956)

It's almost cruel to resurrect this track, although there's a kind of compelling awfulness to it. Probably the classic early Pop song, this was a record-company attempt to score a hit with a 'race record' and as such it thoroughly personifies the Pop tendency to render a 'lite' version of other genres. The quick cover version by white artists of a hit 'race' record was standard practice in the early 50s and many black artists like Big Joe Turner (*Rock Around the Clock*) were sadly trumped in the money stakes by blander white artists like Bill Haley.

Pat Boone was often called upon to record cover versions of hit 'race' records, and along with *Tutti Frutti* he had hits with a number of other songs originally sung by black artists, including Fats Domino's *Ain't That a Shame*, Ivory Joe Hunter's *I Almost Lost My Mind*, and Big Joe Turner's *Chains of Love*. Boone's remakes of these great songs aren't really even R&B or rock 'lite' – they are just 'lite'. His version of *Tutti Frutti* is one of the few tracks I've included in this section of the book that isn't readily available on legal download programmes like iTunes (although you can source it pretty inexpensively – see the Resources section). I've included it, however, because I think it not only has some historical interest in terms of vocal style, but it is also particularly demonstrative of what kind of terrible consequences follow when an artist just can't adapt their style to their material. Consequently I thought it worth including for those willing to track it down – but be warned: it's pretty awful!

Where Little Richard's original recording was an inspired piece of impassioned expression, this production relies on the bland sound of Pat Boone's voice, which gives us time to focus on the song itself. This turns out to be a pretty high-risk strategy in the case of *Tutti Frutti*, because the song is not strong enough to stand on its own. The lyrics are insipid unless delivered with a great energy and a sexually charged innuendo.

It's hard not to feel that Boone is a bit embarrassed at being caught so spectacularly off his usual middle-of-the-road Pop-ballad turf. He is incapable of approaching the song with the kind of explosive energy that made Little Richard's version so memorable. Boone makes no attempt to alter his usual style apart from trying to compress his finishes and stick rigidly to a kind of speech voice quality. On the occasional 'whoo' sounds he is so uncomfortable with the improv that he misses his pitch every time. If you listen to Boone in his natural milieu (easy listening Pop ballads like *April Love*) you can actually admire his kind of smoothness. He always employs a very 'sung', rather schooled sound – it's as pleasant as can be, if never remarkable at all. He swings easily between neutral thick- and thin-fold sounds, never working outside the low effort-level range. He usually exhibits a kind of bland fluidity, but *Tutti Frutti* just baffles him completely and the listening experience is an embarrassing one – a bit like hearing your Granny try an Eminem cover.

'TOXIC' – BRITNEY SPEARS (2004), AND 'WHAT YOU WAITING FOR' – GWEN STEFANI (2004)

Pop seems to break down into a number of categories, but to my ear the most distinguishable are the Pop dance and Pop ballad. These two tracks are both good examples of the really modern twist on Pop dance sound – a sound that probably had its beginnings in Little Eva's *Locomotion* or Chubby Checker's *The Twist*. Pop dance songs usually rely more on instrumental 'hooks' or unusual production than on sung hooks. With *Locomotion* it was the driving saxophone line and with *The Twist* it was the repetitive 'around and around' chorus and the great dance groove of the track. You can hear that as a postmodern version of this kind of Pop, *Toxic*, while wearing all manner of 'street-cred' style elements, is nevertheless a no-holds-barred big Pop production that sells an instrumental hook in the strings line. It's so overproduced that Britney (and indeed the melody) barely gets a look in. When she does sing, there's not a lot of room for her – she's almost crowded out by that string line and a heavy synth bass sound – so she really makes the best of her opportunities. She runs through a lot stylistically and although there's really no chance for her to stray from melody at all she works hard to give all the phrases here some shape and interest with distinctive onsets and mild bends in note attacks mid-phrase. With few exceptions (opening verse), the voice has been recorded many times over and fed through electronic filters and overall, when she does sing, she wisely keeps it very simple although she provides variation in the effort-level throughout.

She begins in a kind of Twangy thin-fold with both voiced and unvoiced Creak onsets. She follows with a thin-fold/Aspirate mix and then waits until the 'toxic' chorus to really come into the voice – and in these sections alone do we really hear a nice neutral thick-fold sound. She switches with ease between these thin- and thick-fold qualities and she has great ease in the really high note sounds that come in about midway, but we never get any high-effort-level qualities; the high effort we hear comes entirely from the instrumental track. We get a lot of different sounds from her, which makes the vocal a great match to the ambitious amount of sound overall. The Creak-into-whisper is Britney's stock in trade and as a sound it goes well with her cultivated sex-kitten image. It's a really clever production, designed to get us dancing and if you can't hum the tune afterwards, you recognise the string-line melodic hook immediately. All the breaks are given over to strange instrumental invention and, towards the end, a strangely '60s-sounding guitar Twang. There's little room for sustain here and nothing whatever, apart from her love of Creak onset and Creak finish (particularly at the end of the song), to distinguish Britney's voice, so she exploits that sound. As with all good Pop dance numbers, we respond to the song (and here, the production) much more than we do to the voice, and there's no particular emotional pull for the listener.

Like *Toxic*, Gwen Stefani's *What You Waiting For* is a very heavy production with so much going on that it's surprising how much Stefani manages to pack in, in terms of style choices. The song's hook revolves around the clock metaphor and apart from the heavy 'tick-tock' choruses, the whole track moves forwards relentlessly in keeping with the message of time both pressing and running out on us. This pace pretty nearly dictates the even phrase-placement throughout, and some of the phrases come in so neatly on top of one another that you know the recording process involved some 'cut and paste'. Sustain is rare here, and when Stefani does use it, it's very brief.

Stylistically, the most interesting thing about this recording is the quick and skilful changes of voice quality. Within the first 50 seconds she goes through at least five qualities. The first four lines are the only gently 'sung' sounds in the piece, using unvoiced Creak onsets, a slightly Twangy thin-fold and Aspirate onsets to create a kind of contemplative mood. This is followed (after the clock sounds) with a seven-line verse that features: (1) very Twangy thin-fold sound and Flip onsets, (2) neutral thick-fold that has a slight

Elongated quality mixed in, (3) neutral thin-fold, (6) neutral thick-fold and (6) a high, fluttery thin-fold with quick vibrato. There is little sustain in the verse, phrase placement is even and the finishes are largely compressed. Note attack features slight bend throughout, which helps to keep some sense of musicality going throughout this rushed and layered first section. By the time we've made it through the track, we've gone through quite a list of stylistic choices which, along with the overall pace and production of the piece, feel rather dizzying. It's hard to say what the song adds up to overall – perhaps just a successful attempt to give stress a dance groove? The lyrics aren't impressive and the set of the lyric to what melody line can be heard is often rather clumsy, but with its catchy tick-tock hook, the song has real appeal in that classic Pop dance way. And Stefani's performance is both clever and perfectly matched to the varied sounds in the track.

'SHE'S THE ONE' – ROBBIE WILLIAMS (1998) AND 'LEAVE RIGHT NOW' – WILL YOUNG (2003)

If you managed to find that Pat Boone track, you'll be relieved to be brought up to date with *She's the One*, which is a beautifully crafted Pop ballad that suits Williams' voice well. The lyrics are relatively inane – never a bad thing in a Pop song, especially if the melodic 'hook' is memorable. He has much more voice than you actually hear here – he's deliberately mixing quite a lot of Aspirate quality in the verses, which he keeps light. He finishes his phrases with either compression or a mild bend and then jumps quickly up a semi-tone and half down to ease out of the line. There's little sustain in these opening verses. He hardens the tone just slightly in the middle-8, which sounds a bit Twangier and gives this driving middle section a little bite. But the great majority of the song is delivered with a low effort-level. He uses only these two voice qualities for the song and the switch between the qualities is not extreme. The phrases are very evenly weighted, and there's nothing remarkable about their shape. There's very little improvisation until the end and even here, the melodic variations are slight and repetitive. He ups the effort-level in this final section with some mild vocal constriction to give the piece a more sincere Rock sound, but he never really relinquishes control enough to make this late move convincing. This allows the *song*, rather than the vocalist, to be the centre of our attention. Perhaps the overall emotional effect of the recording is enhanced if you have some knowledge of the Robbie Williams persona (like the few really superstar Pop singers, Williams has been smart about building his public image), and you feel attracted to it as so many of his fans are. But in truth, nearly any good singer could make a hit of this song if given adequate airplay – it's an easygoing, memorable piece, but it certainly doesn't have a strong emotional pull because it sounds like the calculated hit that it is. It would take either a great and/or unique voice – I can just about hear what Rod Stewart could do with it – to transform this song into something that might evoke a heartfelt emotional response.

Will Young is described on Amazon as having 'housewife appeal', which is probably both a little hard and absolutely accurate. But *Leave Right Now* is a great Pop track. It's not a highly varied vocal performance by any means; most of the song is delivered in his standard Twangy thin-fold sound, although he gets a bit of aspiration into the mix in the first verse. The first chorus is the same vocal quality but with a bit more saturation in the sound. The verse is where the lyric shows vulnerability, which is why the lighter tone works well. In the second verse, which is much more about his wounded soul, there is just the hint of a flip sound mid-phrase which lends to that sense of woundedness, and as he comes into the bridge where he talks about trembling in someone's arms, we get a little trembling sort of improv pattern on the final word. But apart from these really small stylistics, the phrase weight and placement of the verses is even, the phrases have no particular shape to them – there is no sustain and most finishes are compressed. The choruses aren't distinguished from the verse sounds much, but he has a nice kind of ease with the 'hook' line about leaving. This is where the song finally picks up a bit of energy and melody, and although he doesn't do anything adventurous with the phrasing, he does ease and stretch it just slightly in order to bring some relief from the straight sound of the verses. He takes this just a little further by the time we get to the middle-8 section, he pulls the phrase all around the beat and his note attack includes much more bend. Although it's very subtle you can also hear a bit of mild Constriction and even a very mild Rumble, all of which add up to a kind of R&B 'lite' sound. It's not overwhelming at all, but again, it brings us some relief after the pretty straight delivery up until this point. We get a bit more energy on the song where he employs some (not terribly adventurous) improv and some variation in the phrase placement. Again, the impression is of a kind of low-calorie R&B, and it allows us to focus on the song rather than on the artist. And as it's a really well crafted song, that's not a bad outcome.

Both the Robbie Williams and the Will Young songs achieve just what Pop ballads should – I defy you to listen more than once and not feel compelled to sing the choruses yourself afterwards.

SUMMARY

All this emphasis on production/song rather than on voice may make Pop singing sound easy – but as mentioned earlier, I find it one of the hardest styles of all to teach. It requires a number of things that can be difficult to isolate and describe; consequently it's particularly difficult to feel like you can get a handle on the style. There is a wide range of artists who fall into the Pop category, but I think they all share certain style qualities:

1. An overall 'sung' sound – Pop singers tend to have *good* voices (which means pleasant timbre and tone, good pitch, flexibility, accuracy), which are almost never *unique* voices.
2. While there is a wide range of stylistic elements employed in Pop music, those elements are usually used to create a kind of middling effort-level. This means that while the really high effort-level voice qualities (Belt, Twang) are employed in Pop, the neutral qualities are much more often heard.
3. The onset and releases generally employed are of the low- to mid effort-level variety: Flip, Simultaneous, Aspirate, Creak. Vibrato fades are common in Pop music and they do much to give Pop that really 'sung' sound.
4. Improvisation is almost always evident, but it is rarely of the extended Jazz or Gospel type. When you do hear Pop singers who employ extended improvisational patterns, the listening experience is usually one more closely associated to Rhythm & Blues (albeit a kind of R&B 'lite' – Mariah Carey and Celine Dion come immediately to mind). Pop improv consists more often of small additions to the front or back of a phrase – often very quick, usually no more than one or two additional notes.
5. Phrase placement is often very even, but also often just behind the beat. There is never great play or variation in placement of the kind you would hear in Jazz vocal, but neither is the 'easy' looseness of Pop well-served by coming in right on the downbeat too often – unless it's a Pop dance tune.
6. There is a sinuousness and ease to the shape of phrases, often created through dynamic variations within a phrase, well-judged – usually gentle – note bends, variation in onsets and finishes and a lot of small melodic 'adjustments'. These adjustments are not really like improvisation, since they usually serve to just 'ease' a straight melody line and give it a little more shape.

I've learned that it's much easier to approach teaching Pop style if a singer has spent time working on Blues, Jazz and Gospel first. Because these earlier styles are so much easier to delineate in terms of the elements that make them up, they allow a singer who has spent some time working through them to subsequently explore those elements in the kind of lighter way that Pop demands. Work on Blues should give you a good sense of how to occasionally find the raw, more spoken sound that can sometimes be employed by braver Pop artists like Stefani. Work on Jazz style can go a long way towards finding that sinuous, flexible sound through play of phrase-placement and improvisation. Work on Gospel style should lend some ease and confidence in the lighter kind of Pop version of R&B numbers, and also give some increased confidence in extended improvisation. If you've worked your way through all these areas with real dedication, you will ultimately find Pop style coming rather naturally, as long as you make sure your effort-level stays fairly middling and your tone is pleasant throughout.

THE INTERVIEW
Paul McCartney

Perhaps the most versatile popular singer of all time, Paul McCartney's career is now into its fifth decade, and his voice is as strong as ever. There are few singers who perform with quite his abandon and bravery who can say as much. In preparation for this book, I wanted to find someone whose career has stood that test of time, and whose voice is still (despite the demanding and extended work he has put it through) in great shape. It strikes me that he is part of a generation of singers (Rod Stewart, Tina Turner, Tom Jones, Mick Jagger, *et al*) who began singing in the late '50s/early '60s and are still going strong. Singers of a prior generation didn't have the chance to sustain their careers in the spotlight in quite the same way, and it's hard to say if many singers of this generation will have that chance. But it isn't only the resilience and longevity of McCartney's career that should be of interest to us – he is also able to inhabit style in a remarkably flexible way, while still retaining everything about his sound that is unique.

Early in the Beatles' career he was singing songs as diverse as *Long Tall Sally* (a cover of Little Richard's Rock hit) and *Til There Was You* (a sentimental Broadway ballad from Meredith Wilson's *The Music Man*). He still regularly switches effortlessly between his trademark Rock ballad sound (*Michelle, Yesterday,* The *Long and Winding Road, Eleanor Rigby*) and his hard Rock voice (*I'm Down, Jet, I Want to Hold Your Hand, Got to Get You into My Life, Back in the USSR*) and that other, sort of middle-of-the-road sound that seems to have grown out of British Music Hall (*When I'm Sixty-Four, Penny Lane*).

Perhaps nowhere else is his versatility so evident as in two of his later albums: *Flaming Pie* (1997) and *Run Devil Run* (1999). The first was seen by many as the most musically satisfying and complex work he has done since the demise of the Beatles, and the second was a particular challenge that he decided to set for himself in covering a handful of relatively obscure early Rock songs.

In the following interview I wanted to try and get to the heart of how Paul McCartney sees himself as a vocalist, and to see if I couldn't get him to reflect a little on what makes his voice so versatile and how he has managed (where so many others haven't) to retain both the quality and the range of his voice throughout such a long career. Like many practitioners, his first response is always to say that he doesn't reflect on things – he simply does them. But in the course of our afternoon, I was surprised at how much he had to say (despite his repeated insistence that he doesn't think about such things!) about vocal confidence, about the relationship between confidence and sound, between writing and style, between mimicry and finding your own sound, and about singing and playing while performing. He talked a great deal about how listening played an essential part in his own vocal development, about the continued curiosity he has in listening to other artists, and about the breadth of his own evolving musical tastes and knowledge.

Perhaps the thing that struck me most during the interview was that although he is deeply suspicious of analysis, his own natural analytical bent was always evident. I think in many ways his style has grown out of much thinking, listening, imitating and analysing. But as he would insist – a great performance comes when you can *let all of that go and just concentrate on what you want to communicate with the song.*

The interview

Singing has much to do with confidence, and I think for most singers there comes a moment when they actually find the confidence to believe that they can think of themselves *as* a singer – or that they find the confidence to sing in public. Can you tell me when you think you first realised you were a singer?

I guess when I was a young kid. I used to sing along with records. I could hold a tune and I think that's when I realised. It wasn't so much when I was in school; it was more at home, singing along with records or the television.

Was there a particular moment when somebody validated you for doing that – did someone actually say something like 'your voice is nice' or did you come into your own sense of confidence about singing?

I think it was always in my own head. And I suppose getting a record contract was the first validation.

And what about family – any musical influences?

Family – yeah, my dad would be the one. He would teach us harmony and things. He would say 'that's the harmony to that' and he would probably have said 'well, you haven't got a bad voice' but he would never give me too much praise – he was frightened of me getting big-headed.

You've always had a versatile voice and I've always thought of you as the 'hard Rock' singer of the Beatles. You probably do know that a number of voice teachers might counsel you quite strongly against making some of the noises you make when you sing?

Yeah – I'm sure.

And they might say that you could damage your voice doing some of the things you do.

Yeah ... and you shouldn't smoke either! I used to smoke Senior Service without [filter] tips *and* sing Little Richard.

What was your habit – what would you say was the highest number of cigarettes you would smoke in a day?

Forty a day. But the great thing about Rock and Roll is that none of us know anything about singing or else we probably couldn't do half of what we do. I don't know anything about singing at all. I didn't take lessons – I just knew people I liked and I would attempt to mimic them, just like a monkey would in the jungle.

So you were starting with imitation.

Yeah. I think everyone does. I started with imitation, definitely. I started with Elvis Presley – for me, if I sing ballads I think I'm Elvis Presley. Not so much these days – these days I think I'm Paul McCartney! But I used to think I was being Elvis Presley and if I sang high, raucous stuff I thought I was being Little Richard.

I'd like to come back to some of the influences, but I wonder if you could tell me first if you've ever had any vocal problems – any difficulties with recurring hoarseness, or loss of range or anything like that?

No. Well – once. Once when we were in the middle of a tour and I hadn't had any time to recover. I didn't really need to recover – I mean, with the Beatles it didn't seem to make much demand because we had shorter sets – we only did half-hour sets which seems ludicrously short now and if we were angry we only did 25 minutes! And there were two singers – well three singers, but mainly two of us, so in half an hour I only had a maximum of a quarter of an hour's work per night and if George and Ringo both did a song it was even less than that. And so I never really had any problems to speak of. Now it's two hours a set and generally speaking I'm the main vocalist, because generally speaking most people want to hear me singing instead of the other guys in the band. The last tour we did, Hamish from the Average White Band, he would do one number and help me on the vocals but I was still singing for two hours. Which is more than a two-hour opera or musical because at least they've got other characters! But I've found that in doing the show, the main thing I've had to do is realise how long it would take me to recover. And I started to realise that what I should mainly do is have a day off in between shows. In the Beatles there were no problems because I had all these others singers – well, mainly John. But it was short sets and in the actual Beatles concerts there were never more than about 20 minutes of singing. In the Hamburg stuff we did, occasionally we did long hours but again, it was shared with the other guys. So the most difficult time for the voice has been more recently because along with longer sets and being the only one singing, I'm older. But in actual fact, I don't know enough to be worried. So for instance, on the last tour I would do a sound check, which would be about an hour's length and then have a few hours off and then do a two-hour show. So it's about three hours' singing a day with a couple of hours off in between and in fact it's all okay as long as I took a day off after-wards. I would be all raring to go on the day afterwards. The biggest problem I've found is talking after a successful gig – I'd be talking away – ' yeah, it was great, yeah, have a drink, yeah, I loved the way that went, oh did you see that person on the ground', etc. etc., and that was what did my voice in – it wasn't so much the singing – it was the sort of late-night partying and talking a lot about how much fun we had. So I used to have to sort of say, okay you talk – I'll just say yeah or whatever.

When you lost the voice for a little while, how long did it last?

It was actually very short – it was in Pittsburgh – and it was only one day and we still did the show, so it wasn't actually like I lost my voice.

And that's the longest you've ever lost your voice or had severe hoarseness?

Yeah.

No illnesses?

No.

Have you ever had your voice 'scoped'?

No. You know, I'm not that fussed. I just feel like I've been blessed with a gift and I don't want to look at it that much – it's like, you know, it just might vaporise? It might just disappear the more I find out about it so I don't really look too much. I just enjoy it.

Have you ever had any training of any kind?

No. I'm self-trained.

Have you ever noticed changes in sound, like the tone 'scratching' a bit or any change in the actual range that you can sing in?

Normally my voice sounds just like I want it to. To this point – touch wood – it seems to be just what I want it to be. I think it's a lot to do with practice and I'm pretty confident, which is due to my success and I have practised a lot. All those Beatles tours – Hamburg was every day, some days for eight

hours, most days for three or four, but always every day. Playing and singing became second nature. So I think that helps me now to this day. If I would show up and do the Cavern we would have one quick rehearsal on the day at Cavern and I would just go straight on.

And that was two hours?

Cavern? No, that was shorter. But the biggest difficulty was in Pittsburgh. I arrived at the sound check and started to do a song that had some falsetto in it but I couldn't get up into that high range. I thought uh-oh, this is a bit difficult, so I kept on with the sound check, thinking it would just right itself, but it didn't. So I got two voice specialists around. One who just sort of took a look and didn't do much and I didn't think was any good. He just sort of looked at my larynx and said right, you've got a sore throat, mild laryngitis and here's a potion, which didn't really help much. And I had a back-up guy, who they said somebody else had used and had good effect with and he did a bit more ultrasonic treatment on the throat and he did visualisation: 'imagine there's a white light coming in the top of your head and it's coming around and down and surrounding your larynx and it's feeling better' – it was almost like a mild hypnosis kind of thing. And that had enough effect for me to say okay, I'll try and do the show. But the funny bit was, we were in Pittsburgh and we'd played Detroit the night before. And my big opener to the show was always 'good evening people of New York!' or wherever we were – a cheap trick – and you're off on to the music. And this night I was actually thinking of nothing but my throat and I was on autopilot and I was thinking 'will my throat hold out' and I normally don't give it a thought. I was thinking too much about it. So we did our first number, I got by okay, I scraped through, now came the time for my big announcement, and we're in Pittsburgh, and you know what I'm going to say, and I said: 'People of Detroit!' and there was a beat – no reaction at all – and I said 'People of Detroit!' – still no reaction and I said 'You are *NOT* people of Pittsburgh' and then they roared. But I was just distracted thinking about my throat.

Well, your endurance is impressive and you've obviously enjoyed great vocal health during your career. I wonder if we could talk about aesthetics a bit. I've been really interested in listening closely to some of the vocal choices you make – I've been listening a lot to *Run Devil Run* and *Flaming Pie*. In aesthetic terms, do you have icons in your head in terms of who is a 'good' singer?

Well, it depends on what style. Elvis Presley, Little Richard in those kinds of styles. R&B, well, for this year it's Nat King Cole who is, for me, the greatest. I love him. But I also love Fred Astaire. So when I started up, Elvis Presley and Little Richard – or Jerry Lee Lewis, the more sort of manly, somewhere in the middle kind of voice. Or Fats Domino, Ray Charles for a completely different, unique and husky kind of R&B voice. Marvin Gaye just for a beautiful voice, Smokey Robinson for a kind of falsetto-type voice, Bob Dylan for a quirky, personality type of voice, unique kind of voice but for this year I'm listening to a lot of Nat King Cole [he does a great impression of Nat King Cole singing *When I Fall in Love*] I think it's just great – so controlled, so musical, and it's just so effortless. And a big sound for no effort, which I'm always impressed by. I think microphones like lack of effort. I think a microphone diaphragm, if you scream into it very loud it kind of closes down a bit. I know this from making records. So you get a smaller record even though you're singing louder, but if you go to a mic and sing softly it opens up a bit and you get a bigger record. I think that's part of Nat's secret – his mic technique.

And what, in your mind, is a 'bad' voice?

Oh I don't know – just people who don't sing in tune really. Or with very, very wide vibrato. Sounds like starting a car up. I don't really think about bad voices – I just ignore them.

Could you categorise your voice?

I would categorise it as a 'wide-ranging voice'.

And is there one particular style that you think you're most at home in – perhaps ballad singing or Rock singing?

No – I like too many types of things – I'm a Gemini so I like a lot of different things. So I enjoy doing a Rock and Roll album and I enjoy doing ballads and then I don't think of *I'm Down* as any better or worse than *Yesterday*. Although they're completely different styles.

In your head then you feel pretty free about what you're willing to try?

Very free.

Because what you do is quite rangy.

Well, see, I still don't know my range – that's an interesting point. Sometimes I think well, I wonder if I can get this? And it's only by trying it out loud – I've got to do it full tilt – it's got to be right out – that's the only way I know whether I can get something or not.

Do you have a sense that your range has changed as you've grown older?

I keep expecting it to – I don't actually think it has much.

Did your range grow at all in your early or late 20s?

I don't know. I don't really remember. But I think I can get deeper notes now. But on a good night, it's still pretty much what it's always been.

Could we talk a bit about quite specific style things you do— I'm interested in how rarely you use vibrato and actually how often you do what I would call 'legit' ballad singing. Legit ballad singing usually ends with a kind of vibrato fade that eases us out of the sustain. It's not something you do often – is that a conscious choice?

My kind of people don't like it. My tribe don't like vibrato – we think it's a fake, to cover up like it is in string playing, because you don't know exactly where the note is, so you 'vib' either side of it. People like Jeff Lynn, who I work with, really hates vibrato. Notice that the Beatles didn't do much of it. We used pretty much good straight notes, because there's something honest about it.

Does that make sustain difficult sometimes? What you often do is fall off a note, or use a compressed note-ending or occasionally what I call a Creak finish. Interestingly you do very few Creak onsets, which is unusual because most ballad singers do a lot of these.

Just makes me unique, you see.

The most common things you use are what I would call compressed endings or falling off a note, which are Rock-style finishes. Does this have anything to do with mistrust of vibrato – do you think you are consciously suppressing it?

I think to be honest I don't actually like thinking about singing when I'm doing it. Like a friend said to me once, if you're painting never think you're going to paint a masterpiece because it stymies you – you get nervous about this masterpiece you think you're going to paint. So to me everything I like is often a surprise – I like to surprise myself. So I don't really think when I'm singing. I try and just think about communicating with an audience or with a person who's listening to the record. For instance people ask me, well, is it a head voice or a chest voice and I still don't know what that means and I don't want to know what it means. I'm sure I've got a head voice somewhere, or a chest voice, don't I? People say to me what bass strings do you use and I say 'long shiny ones'. I think I'm trying to get an emotion over to people, so I'm thinking more about an emotion because I think the more I think about singing when I'm doing it, the worse I sing. I think it's like riding a bike. In abstract thinking, the more thought you put into it – well, think of Jackson Pollock who used to just drop paint to remove himself from the process – so he'd throw the paint to remove himself. The sheer act of throwing the paint to create line or somebody like DeKooning here [pointing to painting on his wall]. If you *tried* to paint the way he does it would come out all wrong. I admire that kind of thing in singing. That famous director's line about 'throw it away' or 'have fun with it', I think that's what art's about. Once you've prepared to a good reasonable stage then I think it's time to throw everything out of the window and then just go do it.

To be fair, though, you started at a point that many people don't. If you're a young singer just getting started and you don't naturally have the kind of versatility you've always enjoyed – you'll have to do a bit of thinking, won't you?

Yes – when you're learning, yes, you have to think. But once you've done your practice, your learning, you want to be at the point where you don't have to think about it.

If we go back to the ballad sounds on *Flaming Pie* – particularly *Some Days* and *Calico Skies* – were you aware of the great difference in the ballad sound between these two songs – was that a very conscious thing, do you think?

No, not really.

Was the difference in the sound about an emotional choice, then?

I think it comes when I write it. When I write a song I suit the voice to whatever I'm doing when I write it. When I was writing *Calico Skies* it was all based around that little riff. And I think I fell in with that. I was thinking that the riff was little-ish, so I needed a little sound in the voice. I made the voice sympathise with what the musical backing was.

In *Run Devil Run* there's some extraordinarily free improvisation – do you feel freer in a sense when you're doing cover versions of songs?

Yeah – I always envy people who cover my stuff because I always feel that I have to lay down the song properly as it should be. I then think it's kind of nice for people who come later. Because everyone knows the tune, say, of *Hey Jude*, so then Wilson Pickett can come along and sing something entirely different. When you listen to him, I mean those aren't my notes at all – that's not how *Hey Jude* goes. But we know what he's doing. And I can never have a go at that with my own songs because I'm the one who's got to tell the world how *Hey Jude* goes.

It's interesting to hear you say that – maybe that's related to your diction. You may be aware that even in the hard Rock stuff, your diction is very clean. Much cleaner than most hard Rock singers. And when you are doing someone else's song, maybe that's when you feel free to relax the diction a bit. On the Fats Domino song on *Run Devil Run* – *Coquette* – you actually let the diction slide a little bit and you do some improv. Melodic improv is rare on your own stuff.

Yeah – but there we know the tune. It's been laid down by so many, so whoever comes after – after the one who had that job of laying down the tune, or drawing the map – those of us who come after in a way have a slightly freer job.

So if you'd been a singer who'd never written any of the songs you've sung, do you think you'd be a different singer?

Might be, yeah. Yeah, I could have got much more into what my voice is. For me my voice is just part of the whole thing. Just part of it all. The writing song, the accompaniment, I mean – take a song like *Blackbird*, it's 50/50 accompaniment to vocal. That accompaniment is very important – *Blackbird* almost doesn't work if you just do chords to it. It's quite different. So to me that's a good thing. I think if I didn't play instruments, and didn't write, all my attention would just be on what my voice was and I'd start to think that I'd have to know about it more. I would maybe have to do a bit of work on it. And also attitude – I think some people who don't do it all develop attitudes. Like I think Liam Gallagher – I've only just realised he doesn't write stuff and I knew he didn't play an instrument, so I think for him developing some kind of performing attitude is important.

Perhaps that's part of what he has to sell – a kind of defiant 'Rock' attitude?

Yes – otherwise he'd just be standing there twiddling his thumbs all the time because the rest of us have got chords to think about while we sing. One of the things I like in *Run Devil Run* was that I played the bass part as I sang and that made me feel free.

That's interesting, because I would have thought that you would feel less free trying to sing while having to play bass. Would it not have been a freer thing to have sung over the top of the bass track you recorded earlier?

No – it's a freedom that is like not looking too hard at a thing while you're doing it. The more you look at it, the more you tighten up. The more you think about a thing the more nervous you get. With *Run Devil Run* I was new to those songs – I don't think I'd actually sung any of them before. I knew them all but I hadn't sung them. And I just decided that I was going to do it pretty much always in the key that the original artist had sung it in – I think only one or two were different. And I did have just one moment of panic on the Sunday night before the Monday morning session – I thought not only do I not know if I can sing these songs, but I also had been grieving for a year and hadn't sung for a year.

So you hadn't sung at all for a year before going into the studio?

Nothing for a whole year, so on the Sunday night I thought – this is gonna be interesting. If it's anything like Pavorotti, well, on the Monday morning I won't be able to sing. Because I really hadn't done anything – not even warmed up for a whole year. So I had a moment's worry when I thought, wow, this really might not work, I might have to say 'sorry everybody, better go home'. But I knew I'd only booked a week in the studio so I thought well, that wouldn't be too bad. So that was a bit of panic and I knew I'd never sung these songs before so I thought I wonder if I can do it.

So did you warm up on the Monday morning?

No. So then the other thing was ooh – I also don't know the bass parts to these – so I thought what a mine of information I am *not*. And I am going to meet up with these people [the session musicians] **– two of whom I've not met before – and I'm going to meet them from 10 to 10:30 and we're going to start work at 10:30 and I've got two songs to do before lunch. So I thought this is interesting. And I just dove into it head first. Met the guys I didn't know, found we got on fine. Gave them a real quick idea of what we were going to do – I showed them the song. We started at 10:30 and I said does anyone know this song – it was a song called *Fabulous* that I'd heard on a fairground when I was a kid – and they all said no, so without a warm-up I just said 'it goes like this'. I showed them on guitar just the basic riff and sang and they all went yeah, okay, we've got it and I got on bass and we just recorded. And that was the way we did the whole week – there were no warm-ups or anything, it was just dive right in.**

Is that something that you're used to doing? Do you usually warm up?

No. Not at all.

Can I ask when you're doing that hard Rock sound – are you aware at all of what you're doing?

No – I used to say about doing Little Richard stuff, I used to say to myself I just have to jump out of the top of my head. That's as much as I know about it. It's no good doing Little Richard with a pinched little voice, you actually have to go for it – I can't show you here, it would be too loud. It's like play-ing bagpipes – you can't play them indoors. To me you can't do it in a small room. To me, well, it's just a matter of jumping out of the top of my head really – it's something that I just know how to do.

And you're not aware of any extra tension or muscle work going on when you sing that way?

Not really, no – I just sort of know the voice that I do that was based on imitating Little Richard when I was a teenager, when he first came out and I got what was my impression of Little Richard down. And if you listen to *Long Tall Sally* it is a pretty good impression of Little Richard. And then I started to get my own style. Something like *I'm Down* was a bit more me than Little Richard. But it definitely started off with mimicking. But once I had an imprint of like the mimic thing my head and body knew how to do it; knew what muscles to use – I just knew how to mimic that voice. I couldn't really begin to analyse it. It's as if I play a role and all the chops in the voice go with it.

After singing that kind of hard Rock, do you find it hard to go into a ballad sound?

I don't think so. I do that on stage and it's quite good – it's a relaxing sort of pacing thing. On stage I'll have two or three loud songs and naturally bring it down a bit just pacing both for the audience and for me. So it all seems to just happen quite naturally. In everything I do the word 'primitive' is always very important. So like I sail a boat; I've never had a boat lesson in my life but I'm not a bad sailor. And when I get out with the sail and the wind I think yeah – primitive man did this. I love that – it touches me. When I paint I think of cave paintings and when I sing it's the same way. I've never had a guitar lesson, I've never had a singing lesson, I've never had a bass lesson. I have had a piano lesson like everyone has – doing scales – but I hated it. I've had quite a few attempts at that during my life and I've always hated it. I think about singing lessons, well, it's all horses for courses, isn't it. Some people sound good when they've had lessons. But I have to say – all the people I've really admired, have not had a lesson in their lives to my knowledge. That may just be something to do with my taste but I think that you will generally that people who are really moving music on – say the early Jazz musicians in New Orleans – these guys generally weren't taught.

So throughout the whole of your life you've never had a singing teacher talk to you or work with you in any way?

No.

Finally – and you've touched on this a bit – are you finding the speaking voice lowering or changing?

No. I'm a bit of a chameleon. Ringo said this to me once – he was explaining it to Barbara – he said 'he's got thousands of voices'. I've always been a mimic – I mimic characters. I do have a lot of characters in my head. And it's the same with singing I think – it's just an extension of all of that. I ring people up on the phone when I'm kidding around and they often don't think it's me.

But when you're just talking in your normal voice – no changes you can detect?

No. Accent has changed – I've lived down here now longer than I lived in Liverpool. But when I go back up there I pick up the accent. Or when I spend even a day in Ireland. But I just can't help it because I always want to belong. I want to communicate.

The thing about the tracks on *Run Devil Run*, at this point in your career, I mean, they sound like *Long Tall Sally* – you seem to still have all the voice now that you had 20, 30 years ago.

That's why I don't want to think about it too much.

But of course that's why I do! I mean, what explains people like you? For those of us who teach singers, it would be interesting to know why some voices, like yours, last well despite the kind of singing you do, which many voice tutors might worry about. No warm-ups, 'jumping out of the top of your head' to sound like Little Richard – you just seem to have an amazingly resilient voice.

Maybe it's something to do with attitude. If in some way I'm happy or focused or really know what I want to sing. No – that's bollocks – with *Run Devil Run* I didn't really know what I wanted to sing. But my dad had a great expression – DIN, Do It Now – that's quite a good one. Just do it. And somehow often in that sheer fact of doing it you find out more about it. I've worked a lot live. And maybe it's to do with confidence – you would have confidence if you'd been in the Beatles!

RESOURCES FOR LISTENING AND READING

If you manage to listen to every song I've used for the analyses in Section Four, you will hear clear examples of every voice quality described in Section Two and every complementary element described in Section Three. I've chosen the songs in Section Four precisely for this reason, although I recognise that there may be a desire to listen further to particular kinds of qualities or elements of style, so along with instructions on how to source everything mentioned in Section Four, I've also included some ideas about how to do further listening. I'm also including some books and websites that I hope you may be interested in but, of course, the list is far from exhaustive.

Finding songs referred to in Section Four

As mentioned earlier, for the most part I've tried to stay with songs easily located on iTunes, and you should be able to purchase all the downloadable songs I've used in the close analyses in this section for around £20. I've also included information for finding those songs that are mentioned but not closely analysed – this will stretch your budget a bit further but you should still be able to keep your full purchase of all the songs listed below at under £35. I've included information for finding music on Amazon (either the US or the UK Amazon – unless otherwise indicated, most of these are available on Amazon.co.uk). This is, of course, a more expensive option, although many of these CDs are available now on the 'new and used' section for purchase through Amazon, which means that I've been able to source some of these CDs for less than £4. Titles marked with a * indicate songs analysed in Section 4.

BLUES
Bessie Smith
* *Gimme a Pigfoot and a Bottle of Beer:* Available on iTunes, also available on CD (*Martin Scorsese presents the Blues: Bessie Smith*) both available on Amazon.co.uk
Down Hearted Blues: Available on iTunes, also available on CD (*Down Hearted Blues*), available on Amazon.co.uk

Robert Johnson
* *Terraplane Blues:* Available on iTunes, also available on CD (*The Complete Collection* [Platinum]), available on Amazon.co.uk

Sonny Boy Williamson
* *Dealing with the Devil:* Available on iTunes, also available on CD (*Bluebird Blues* [Bluebird]), available on Amazon.co.uk

Etta James
* *I Just Want to Make Love to You* and * *At Last:* Available on iTunes, also available on numerous CDs, including *The Best of Etta James* and *At Last* (both available on Amazon.co.uk)

GOSPEL
Five Blind Boys of Mississippi
* *His Eye is On The Sparrow:* Available on iTunes, also available on CD through US suppliers: *20th Century Masters – The Millenium Collection: Best of the Blind Boys of Mississippi* (available on Amazon.com marketplace, Tower-Records.com, and music.barnesandnoble.com)

Aretha Franklin
* *Precious Lord, Take my Hand, part 1:* Available on iTunes and also on CD (Aretha Gospel [Chess]), available on Amazon.co.uk

Mahalia Jackson
★ *Amazing Grace:* Available on CD (*The Essential Mahalia Jackson* [Metro]), available on Amazon.co.uk

JAZZ
Louis Armstrong and Bing Crosby
Now You Has Jazz: Available on CD (*Now You Has Jazz: Louis Armstrong at M-G-M* [Rhino/WEA]), available on Amazon.com

Billie Holiday
Strange Fruit: Available on iTunes

Ella Fitzgerald
A-Tisket A-Tasket: Available on iTunes

Nina Simone
My Baby Just Cares For Me: Available on iTunes

Peggy Lee
Fever: Available on iTunes

Louis Armstrong
★ *You Rascal You:* The version I use for analysis can be found on a CD titled *Louis Armstrong at His Best*, which is available on Amazon.co.uk. You can, however, download a different (still very early) version from iTunes, which is drawn from an album entitled *Blues for Yesterday* and while it is clearly not the same track you will certainly hear all the things discussed in the analysis.

Ella Fitzgerald
★ *Midnight Sun:* Available on iTunes and on CD (*Ella Fitzgerald Sings The Johnny Mercer Songbook* [Polygram]) available on Amazon.co.uk
★ *Lady Be Good* – 1947 version: Available on iTunes and on CD (*The Best of Ella Fitzgerald* [Decca]), available on Amazon.com or Amazon.co.uk as import

Peggy Lee
★ *The Best is Yet To Come:* Available on iTunes and on CD (*I Like Men / Sugar and Spice* [EMI]), available on Amazon.co.uk

Frank Sinatra

★ *In The Wee Small Hours of the Morning:* available on iTunes and on CD (*In the Wee Small Hours of the Morning* [Capitol]), available on Amazon.co.uk

Diana Krall

★ *Almost Blue:* available on iTunes and on CD (*The Girl in the Other Room* [Verve]), available on Amazon.co.uk

Jazz Instrumentalists

As mentioned earlier, along with listening to Jazz singers, it's really important to listen to Jazz instrumentalists as well. It can be difficult sometimes, but trying to sing along with a Jazz instrumental track is great practice for your ear. I find this most helpful when listening to a Jazz instrumental version of a song I know fairly well because it allows me to gain a greater understanding of just how and where they push the boundaries of a piece as written. For that reason I would suggest the following tracks of songs that you may know, but of course there are many, many other resources:

Chet Baker – *You Go To My Head:* available on iTunes and on CD (*Chet Baker: Chet for Lovers* [Verve]) available on Amazon.com

Miles Davis – *Bye Bye Blackbird:* available on iTunes and on CD (*Live at Newport 1958* [Sony]) available on Amazon.co.uk

Buddy Rich, Lionel Hampton, Oscar Peterson – *Willow Weep For Me:* available on iTunes and on CD (Verve Jazz Masters, Vol. 1)

Dizzy Gillespie – *They Can't Take That Away from Me:* available on iTunes and on CD (Odyssey 1945-1952 [Savoy Jazz])

COUNTRY
Hank Williams

★ *Your Cheatin' Heart:* available on iTunes and on CD (*The Best of Hank Williams* [Spectrum]), available on Amazon.co.uk
★ *Hey Good Lookin:* available on iTunes and on CD (*The Best of Hank Williams* [Spectrum]), available on Amazon.co.uk

Tammy Wynette

★ *D.I.V.O.R.C.E.:* available on iTunes and on CD (*The Best of Tammy Wynette* [Epic]), available on Amazon.co.uk

If you want to hear some contemporary Country tracks that retain a traditional vocal sound, I would recommend Kenny Chesney and Deana Carter – both of whom have many tracks available on iTunes.

ROCK

Elvis Presley

★ *Don't Be Cruel:* available on iTunes and on CD (*30 #1 Hits* [RCA]), available on Amazon.co.uk
★ *Heartbreak Hotel:* available on iTunes and on CD (*30 #1 Hits* [RCA]), available on Amazon.co.uk

Little Richard

★ *Tutti Frutti:* available on iTunes and on CD (*The Original British Hit Singles* [Ace]), available on Amazon.co.uk

Paul McCartney

★ *Run Devil Run:* available on CD (*Run Devil Run* [Parlophone]). This is one of the very few examples I've included not available on iTunes, but it's very easily sourced on Amazon.co.uk where you should be able to find the full CD in the new & used section for under £3.

POP

Pat Boone

★ *Tutti Frutti:* available on CD (*Pat Boone at his best* [Pulse]). This is another of the few examples included that is not available on iTunes, but it's easily found on Amazon's new & used section – currently for under £2.50.

Britney Spears

★ *Toxic:* available on iTunes and also on CD (as *Toxic* CD single [Jive]) from Amazon.co.uk

Gwen Stefani

★ *What you Waiting For?:* available on iTunes and on CD (*Love Angel Music Baby* [Polydor]) available from Amazon.co.uk

Robbie Williams

★ *She's the One:* available on iTunes and on CD (*Greatest Hits* [Chrysalis]) available from Amazon.co.uk

Will Young
* *Leave Right Now:* available on iTunes and on CD (*Friday's Child* [BMG]), available from Amazon.co.uk

Books on voice training
There are a lot of books and websites on voice training out there. I recommend these three, which are very different but very useful.

Singing and The Actor by Gillyanne Kayes: although this is very much geared toward Musical Theatre repertoire and style, it includes some really solid technical information on voice production and is a great all-around work on approaching song interpretation for Musical Theatre. (London: A&C Black, 2004), available on Amazon.co.uk

The Contemporary Singer by Anne Peckham: geared towards a more traditional training approach, this is full of great advice for those who want to train on their own, is very clear and includes easy-to-follow practice. (Boston: Berklee Press, 2000), available on Amazon.co.uk

Singing With Your Own Voice by Orlanda Cook: this is a refreshing book that pays no attention to the 'rules'. Full of practical advice on expanding the kinds of sounds you can make. (London: NHB, 2004), available on Amazon.co.uk

Workshops in voice training
There are a number of options for gaining more knowledge about vocal qualities and methods, and for further intensive training in these areas in the UK you might want to try the following. Their language and approach will be slightly different, but you'll learn a lot of useful things for working in contemporary style very quickly.

Vocal Process
You can find much information (and some interesting resources) through their website, www.vocalprocess.co.uk. They offer a number of different courses, from short day-workshops to longer, more intensive training.

Think Voice International
You'll find information on the Estill Method through this group on

www.trainmyvoice.com, and under the News and Events section you'll find opportunities for short-course training in the UK.

Further reading in popular music

Of course there are many, many books in this area but I found the few I'm listing below to be both really useful research and highly enjoyable reading as well.

Escott, Colin, *The Story of Country Music* (London: BBC Worldwide Ltd., 2003)

Guralnick, Peter, *Lost Highway* (Edinburgh: Canongate, 2002)

Guralnick, Peter, *Sweet Soul Music* (Edinburgh: Canongate, 2002)

Guralnick, Peter, *Feel Like Going Home* (Edinburgh: Canongate, 2003)

Miller, James, *Almost Grown: the rise of rock* (London: William Heinemann, 1999)

Oakley, Giles, *The Devil's Music*, second ed. (London: Da Capo Press, 1997)

O'Brien, Lucy, *She-Bop* (London: Penguin Books, 1995)

Websites

Of course, there are lots of websites on popular music and you'll probably have many of your own favourites. If you've not come across these, however, I think you'll find them really useful.

www.thebluehighway.com – there are many Blues websites, but I really like this one. It has great archive material, lots of history, discographies and good links to other sites.

http://gospelhighway.50megs.com/GOSPEL/gospelindex.htm – I wouldn't try this site without a pop-up blocker, but it is a rich vein of information about Gospel music, its tradition and Gospel artists, from the very earliest to contemporary Gospel artists and sounds. A great resource.

www.VH1.com – is a rich resource for music of all kinds that includes a great archive of information, particularly in their 'artists' section, which is not only extensive but is also really well-linked to other sites and information. Click on the Artists A–Z tab and you'll find a wealth of information on nearly every popular music artist you can think, and there is also an extremely valuable discography that includes ALL albums (not just the albums they sell!) – a useful site and you will probably be impressed with how much historical information the site contains.

www.rockhall.com - this is the website for the Rock'n'Roll Hall of Fame, based in Cleveland, Ohio. It's full of interesting information about artists who have been inducted into the hall, but also has some great information on who influenced those artists and you can spend much time in permanent collection pages – particularly on the '500 songs that shaped rock'n'roll' page, where you'll find lots to inspire and interest.

Further listening in vocal qualities and the elements of style

We've covered much of this ground above, and some of the more easy-to-do things I've left out of this last section. Instead, I've tried to include examples below of things that are a little more out of the ordinary and that participants in my workshops always ask for more examples of. Some of these are sounds that are more extreme and perhaps a bit harder to train your ear to hear and to use with skill. I hope you find the following examples both interesting and inspiring.

Aspirate voice quality and onsets/releases:

Norah Jones – *The Nearness of You* (Available on iTunes and on CD: *Come Away With Me* [Capitol]) – The dominant quality here feels like Aspirate, although when you listen closely you can hear that she's often in neutral thin- or thick-fold, but it's really a masterclass in how to use the Aspirate quality to create great intimacy with the listener.

Damien Rice – *Eskimo Friend* (Available on iTunes and on CD: *O* [East West]) – He's using a lot of other qualities, but certainly the dominant quality of opening of the track is Aspirate. He's a real master of moving from quality to quality and especially in moving from thick-fold sound into Aspirate very quickly.

Elongated quality:

Anita Baker – (*Sweet Love* (Available on iTunes and on CD: *Rapture* [Atlantic]) – You can hear right from the first phrase a beautiful switch from thick-fold into Elongated quality, which she uses with great skill at many points in this track. She's working predominantly in thick-fold and Twang (right at the upper end), but it's always been her really skilful use of the Elongated quality that makes this track so memorable to me.

Donny Hathaway – *Someday We'll All be Free* (Available on iTunes and on CD: *A Donny Hathaway Collection* [Atlantic]) – Like the Baker track above, you'll hear a switch from thick-fold into Elongated quality in the very first phrase here. He saves much of his work in this quality at the very lower end of his range (he certainly does that in this track), but as you'll hear in the first two lines of the song he likes to experiment with this sound elsewhere. I think it gives a beautiful, rich and haunting sound to his work.

Twang quality:

Patti LaBelle – *Lady Marmalade* (Available on iTunes and on CD: *School Disco. Com, Spring Term* [Sony]) – She always works predominantly through Twang quality, and in this track even her spoken bits are twangy. As the track progresses the Twang gets more pronounced and sharper – especially following the instrumental break.

Chaka Khan – *Through the Fire* (Available on iTunes and on CD: *Epiphany: the Best of Chaka Khan, vol. 1*) – The last two choruses of this track are great examples of the classic Twang high wail R&B sound. She's in thick-fold and Belt through quite a lot of the song, and you'll hear a bit of Aspirate in the very first verse. But once we're past the instrumental break, she makes great use of that high twanging wail.

Belt quality

U2 – *Pride (In the Name of Love)* (Available on iTunes and on CD: *The Best of 1980–1990* [Island]) – This is a great track for hearing a quick contrast between neutral thick-fold and Belt, which happens between the first two verse and chorus sections. As the track progresses he mixes much more into the last verse section, but you can always sense when he's gone into that beautiful pure Belt.

Whitney Houston – *I Will Always Love You* (Available on iTunes and on CD: *Greatest Hits* [Arista]) – A fascinating track to listen to for voice-quality changes. The first verse is a mix of neutral and Aspprirate qualities and the first chorus is entirely thin-fold. Second verse is predominantly neutral thick-fold and the second and ensuing choruses are pure Belt, from which she flips very skilfully into thin-fold sound from time to time.

The dangerous qualities:

You should be able to hear a variety of Constricted, Creaked and Rumbled qualities as well as their corresponding onsets in the following tracks. You'll notice that the sounds are sometimes mixed and hard to hear in their 'pure' state.

B.B. King – *How Blue Can You Get* (Available on iTunes and on CD: *King of the Blues* [Ace]) – Although there is a very Constricted sound to this track, I think it's a kind of 'Rumbled Constriction' – you can hear that the sound is happening as a kind of combination of stiffening soft palate and that gargle set-up described earlier.

Otis Redding – *I've Been Loving You Too Long* (Available on iTunes and on CD: *Otis Redding Live in Europe* [Warner]) – This is a live version and you get a great sense of the effort in this performance. You can hear a kind of combination of Creak and Constricted qualities in the higher end of the range, growing more urgent and gritty as the track goes on, with great Constricted onsets in the final 'I love you' repeats.

Kenny Rogers – *Lucille* (Available on iTunes and on CD: *Greatest Hits* [Capitol]) – This track has the classic Kenny Rogers sustained Creak sound. He creaks for almost the whole of the first two verses, but loses the sound entirely for the choruses.

Janis Joplin – *Piece of My Heart* (Available on iTunes and CD: *Greatest Hits* [Columbia]) – A classic of extended use of Constricted Blues/Rock tone with just enough clear tones on the early verse to remind you that this was something Joplin chose to do.

Tina Turner – *I Don't Want to Fight No More* (Available on iTunes and on CD: *What's Love Got to Do With It* [Virgin]) – Tina Turner rarely makes a low-energy vocal choice but she's so wise about how she uses her effort. You can hear both Constricted onsets (particularly in the choruses and especially on the 'I' sounds) as well as some carefully judged sustained Constricted sounds in most of the choruses and at the very end of the bridge section. You can also hear a very fast Flip on so many of the phrases, which is the result of so much effort in the vocal.

Nirvana – *Smells Like Teen Spirit* (Available on iTunes and on CD: *Nirvana* [Geffen]) – All of the choruses are great examples of sustained Constricted quality.

COMPLEMENTARY ELEMENTS

You'll hear many of these so commonly that I've only chosen some really extreme examples of the sounds.

Flip:

Patsy Cline – *Your Cheatin' Heart* (Available on iTunes and on CD) – You'll hear a number of interesting choices here, and along with a liberal use of the Flip you'll hear her actually stop what might have been a Flip mid-way and simply use a very edgy Aspirate into the next vowel sound.

Creak:

Enrique Iglesias – *Hero* (Available on iTunes and on CD: *Escape* [Interscope]) – A persistent use of Creak onset!

Des'ree – *You Gotta Be* (Available on iTunes and on CD: *I Ain't Movin'* [Sony]) – A nice mix of Creak onsets and releases.

Pushed release:

For a great example of the extreme form of this release, have a listen to Ruth Brown's early classic *Mama He Treats Your Daughter Mean*, where she employs the finish a couple of times but mostly on the lyric 'Mama' (available on iTunes). It's the same sound you'll hear in Louis Jordan's *Caledonia* or Little Richard's *Lucille*. For a milder form of this finish, listen to Dinah Washington's fabulous *Drinking Again* (Available iTunes and on CD: *Dinah '62* [Roulette]), where she uses it often but it is much more subtle.

Gospel release:

Although it will take a bit more work to track down, there is probably no better demonstration of the power and full emotional charge of the Gospel release than Jennifer Holliday's *And I Am Telling You I'm Not Going*. This recording really is so phenomenal you will find it repays your effort to get hold of it. (It's not on iTunes, sadly, but you can find it on two CDs: *The Best of Jennifer Holliday Millennium Collection* [Universal], and on the soundtrack for the musical *Dreamgirls* [Universal]. Both are available on Amazon.co.uk and the first is available currently available in the new & used section for £3.75. You can probably find other sources, including other legal download programmes.) It's a great example of Gospel release right the way through the track, but it is so rich in other qualities and elements and is such a bold, emotionally charged performance you will find it inspiring in its bravery.

GREAT TRACKS FOR HEARING VOICE-QUALITY CHANGES

The following tracks can be really helpful in learning to identify a lot of the voice qualities and elements we've been looking at because they run through such a number of things both quickly and clearly. Listen a few times – each new listening will bring greater rewards in terms of training your ear to hear both the varieties of voice qualities and the application of the complementary elements of style.

Pop:

Christina Aguilera – *A Voice Within* (available on iTunes) – Great example of how changing voice qualities really quickly can drive up the perceived effort-level and create a lot of style with a very simple melody. Her opening verse is dominated by Creak, neutral thin-fold and Aspirate sounds. The choruses are filled with quick switches from Belt to neutral thin- or thick-fold sounds. As the song progresses and the pitch rises, the Belt gives way to some thin-fold or 'baby' Twang sounds. You'll also hear some light Rumble sounds and some moderate Gospel release sounds as well. Whatever your take on Christina Aguilera, you will probably at least appreciate the amount of things at work in this track.

R&B:

Van Hunt – *Dust (Live)* (available on iTunes) – I love this track because it demonstrates great facility in moving quickly from thin-fold to Aspirate to thick-fold in the opening sections, and then exploring a number of gritty possibilities as the pain of the song grows deeper. Although he has a beautiful voice (which at times seems to come straight out of the classic Motown school), in this song Hunt uses every weapon in his style arsenal to defy any expectation of beautiful singing and to keep the truth of the song foremost as we hear it. From the lighter sounds of the opening verses and choruses, the fast changes from Belt and thick-fold into Creak, thin and Aspirate sound finally lead into a finish that is largely a combination of Belt, 'baby' Twang and sustained Creak that add up in such a convincing way to tell the story of man who is right on the edge.

John Legend – *Ordinary People* (available on iTunes and on CD) – I think the creative way he finishes a sound on this track is just wonderful. The song is about the real grit of a relationship and there's nothing romantic or dreamy in this vision of love. The vocal matches that beautifully. He has a really great voice but he resists 'singing' the song to us here – what he has to say is too important for that. You'll hear a lot of scratch and Creak in the voice quality, which is dominated by thick-fold with some Belt. He begins the song with some traditional vibrato fades but as the track progresses you hear much more in the way of compressed end and often he finishes with a kind of twist on the Gospel release, exhaling strongly on a 'hey' or 'yeah' sound – always putting great energy and weight towards the back of a phrase. Towards the end of the song you can feel the thought and the sound sort of returning back into the singer and although still not 'beautiful', the gritty qualities become softer and more contemplative and he uses more thin-fold sound. Just right for this really remarkable exercise in style and communication.

Jazz:

Rachelle Ferrell – *You Send Me* – This is a great track that really demonstrates the joys of quick quality switches in performance. In the early verses she makes much of her use of Elongated quality and easily pops right out of that sound into a very light thin-fold sound in just the right places on the second verse. There's a little light Creak in the onset from time to time, and typical of Jazz style, she uses a lot of compressed and falling-off-the-note finishes. You hear a lot of Aspirate, thick-fold and Twang in the verses after the instrumental break – basically she quite freely runs through all the qualities and that, along with her free and creative phrase placement means it all adds up to a really satisfyingly playful re-think of the old Sam Cooke classic.

INDEX

SONG INDEX

COPYRIGHT HOLDERS

Precious Lord (Take My Hand)